Slavery
and a
Countess Wear Family:

The Davy Family in Devon and Jamaica

Gillian Allen

Devon History Society
Book of the Year Awards 2025
W. G. HOSKINS AWARD
Joint Winner

ISBN: 978-1-0369-0222-3

Publisher: Gillian Allen, Exeter, UK

CONTENTS

ACKNOWLEDGEMENTS

I am grateful to the Glanville family of Mandeville for giving their support in tracing the Jamaican Davy family, especially to James for his enthusiastic participation and extensive local knowledge. I am also grateful to the Davy family of Western Australia, especially Geoffrey and Primrose, for involving me in their family history expedition to Jamaica and sharing their family history and documents. I thank Devon Development Education and the Legacies of Devon Slavery Connections Group who have been as obsessed as I am in the search for slavery links between Devon and the Caribbean, giving freely of their time and expertise. I also thank Richard and Marjorie-Anne Howe for their help with interpreting old legal documents.

Cover illustrations: Nineteenth century maps showing land divisions in NW Manchester *(Institute of Jamaica)*

Typeset, printed and bound by Short Run Press, Exeter

INTRODUCTION

This is an account of the Davy family of Devon (England) and Jamaica. It focuses on a particular family in their particular locations but attempts to show their place in the international economy. It aims to uncover how a Devon farming family became slave-owners, how they coped and thrived, how slave-ownership may have benefitted their family over the generations and enabled them to participate in British colonial expansion.

I have enquired into the lives and deaths of both the white Davys and their enslaved Africans. I have made particular use of the Slave Registers[1], some of the only records which tell us about the births and deaths of enslaved workers. The idea is to tell a balanced story which recognises that the histories of black and white are not separate but intimately linked through our shared past.

---

1 Former British Colonial Dependencies, Slave Register, 1813-1834; available on Ancestry.com

MY STORY

The Davy story parallels my own. As with the Davys, I started in Countess Wear, an area just south of the city of Exeter in the county of Devon in south west England. I also lived in the parish of Manchester in central Jamaica in the Caribbean as did the Davys. Like the Davys I travelled many times across the Atlantic, though they endured dangerous sea journeys of several weeks while I travelled quickly and comfortably on Air Jamaica.

I am an Englishwoman who lived in Countess Wear then resided in Jamaica for many years and eventually returned to Countess Wear. I was married to a Jamaican coffee farmer, had mixed-race children, and taught physics in a local high school. This left me in the uncomfortable position of having a foot in both camps with the tension that comes from being between cultures that do not entirely like or understand each other – for historical reasons beyond their individual control.

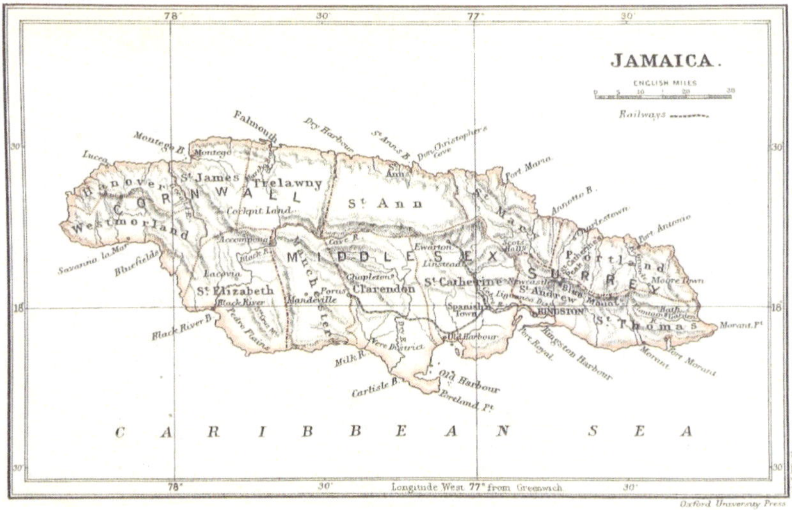

Map of Jamaica (1888) (Stock Photo Alamy)

I had no idea about the history of the parish of Manchester, in central Jamaica, when I lived there, as it does not have the typical sugar plantation history given in history books. I did not know there were ruined estates in the vicinity called Topsham, Heavitree and Wear. But when I returned to Countess Wear I heard a talk by local historian, Geoffrey Harding, who told us about the Davy family's ship-building business on the Exe estuary and their link with Jamaica. This immediately piqued my interest as I had had a teaching colleague in Jamaica called Mrs Davey – could there be a connection despite the difference in spelling? Soon after, the internet started opening up sources of information that were previously unobtainable. A very useful site was jamaicanfamilysearch.com on which genealogist Patricia Jackson made available historical records such as the Jamaican Almanacs, listing slave-owners and their properties. These showed the existence of Topsham, Heavitree and Wear, owned by Davy men, in the parish of Manchester in Jamaica, and the number of enslaved Africans they owned.

But was there a connection to Mrs Davey? I used the on-line Jamaican yellow pages and systematically telephoned all Daveys until I found one who said yes, his grandfather had come from Topsham (the Jamaican Topsham) and he was the brother-in-law of Mrs Davey, the teacher. With this link established I was able to plan a visit.

I set off with my enthusiastic and knowledgeable friend, James Glanville, on a History Adventure in August 2007. This led us to Wear Pen, the nearby St George's church with its many tombstones, Heavitree and Topsham, among other ruined plantation houses. This was all new and amazing to me!

Later, I was contacted by a Davy descendant in Australia who had obtained my email address through a history website. This was Geoffrey Davy – a man keen to trace his family history. Although he knew about his family's Jamaican past, his interest had been

Author searching for the remains of Topsham plantation, Jamaica (Photo by friend of the author)

renewed by the BBC television programme "Who do you think you are?" which was investigating the family history of TV chef, Ainsley Harriott. It showed Ainsley in Jamaica confronting a plaque to John Davy, Geoffrey's great-grandfather, who had 'owned' Ainsley's enslaved ancestor. Geoffrey and his sister, Primrose, were filled with enthusiasm to make the ambitious journey to see places connected with their ancestors in Countess Wear and in Jamaica. This visit took place in 2011. With my guidance, they visited most of the places mentioned in this story and their visits are illustrated in this book. With my help, Geoffrey subsequently wrote a book about his family history based partly on this trip, on which I have drawn heavily for this account[2].

This book is my attempt to put all this Davy history together in a systematic way and to relate it to background issues in Jamaican and British history, with the emphasis on the institution of plantation slavery.

---

2 Davy, G.J.G. (2013). *The Davy family: Gaius 1633 to Ebony Rae 2012.* Exlibris.

PART 1 EARLY HISTORY OF THE DAVY FAMILY IN DEVON

Early history of the Davy family[3]

Gaius Davy (about 1633 to after 1685) is said to have lived at Wylde Court, Hawkchurch, Dorset. He supported the unsuccessful Monmouth Rebellion of 1685 and was forced to flee to escape the reprisals of Judge Jeffreys, reputedly hiding out in Heath Orchard, Pinhoe, on the outskirts of Exeter in Devon. A lead coffin unearthed there in the 1840s when a railway cutting was being dug is suggested to have been Gaius Davy's because it was buried secretly without the usual formalities. The family lost their wealth and became tenant farmers in Pinhoe.

Wylde Court, Hawkchurch (Photo by author)

Gaius' son James (about 1663-1733) made his home at Mere Farm, later incorporated into Whipton Barton Farm, now a cottage at 393 Pinhoe Road, Heavitree, Exeter. He was followed by his son Philip (1701-1752) and later Philip's son, James (1729-1813), who made the move from Heavitree to Countess Wear (at that time called, simply, Wear).

Davy family in Countess Wear[4]

In about 1765, James Davy became a tenant farmer at Wear Barton

---

3 There is no known relationship between this Davy family and other well-known Davys such as Sir Humphry Davy (the scientist from Penzance) or William Davy (the lawyer for James Somerset in the 1771-2 slavery case).

4 This section draws on Ponsford, C.N. (1988). *Shipbuilding on the Exe.* Devon and Cornwall Record Society.

Map of Wear and surrounding areas (Donn 1765; wikimedia.org)

Farm, Countess Wear, on land belonging to John Spicer of Wear House. Wear House is now Exeter Golf and Country Club and the area of Wear Barton Farm is now the Glasshouse Lane council estate. Countess Wear is an area just to the south of Exeter and to the north of Topsham, and is on the edge of the River Exe which, before the advent of the railway, was an important industrial zone using the river for transport. At this time the Agrarian Revolution was in full swing and agricultural methods were improving; adding lime to the soil was one of these improvements. James built lime kilns alongside the Exe, at Mill Road and at Gulpit on Glasshouse Lane, which still exist. James imported limestone from quarries such as at Babbacombe, South Devon, and burnt the stone to make lime. This process also required importing coal. These heavy

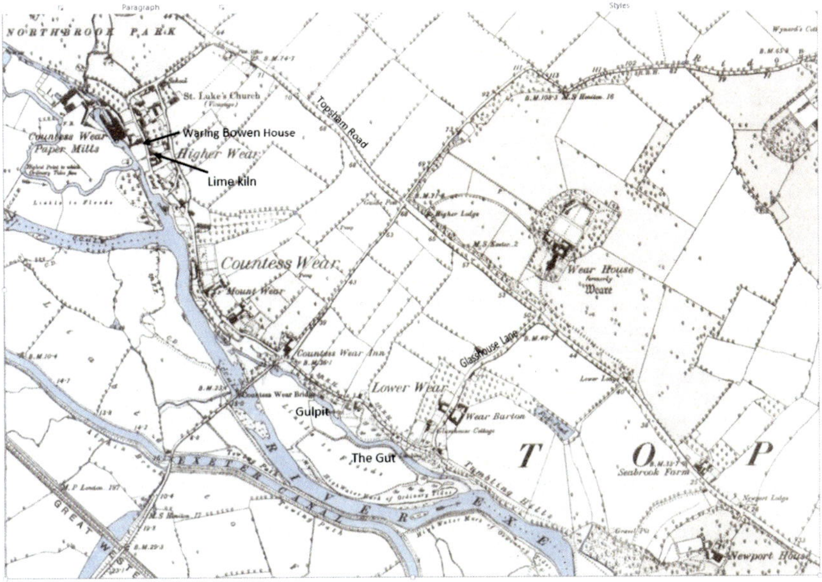

Detailed Map of Countess Wear 1889 (National Library of Scotland)

raw materials were brought up the shallow river by small boats called 'lighters', which would sometimes need to be repaired, so James learned to repair boats too, aided by one of his sons, Robert. The painting overleaf by F. J. Carpenter shows where the lighters brought limestone to the kilns, just visible on the left.

Robert Davy (1762-1862) the shipbuilder

It is Robert Davy, the shipbuilder, who is remembered in Countess Wear and Topsham today. He continued his father's businesses to become *"the largest lime-burner, coal merchant and ship-builder in the West of England. Also he farmed and grazed very extensively; and he did a little in the Newfoundland trade besides selling large quantities of oak timber and bark"*[5]. John Swete called him *"this great Lime*

---

5 Ponsford p.ix.

Painting of Countess Wear (F. J. Carpenter, 1961) (St Luke's church rooms)

Manufacturer, who by spirited enterprise had contributed essentially to the promotion of the Agricultural interests of his Neighbourhood; and at the same time secured to himself an independent fortune"[6]. He built his house, now known at Waring Bowen House, on Mill Road, Countess Wear, in 1789.

Robert, then, was a self-taught shipbuilder. Starting out at the side of the River Exe at the junction with the narrow man-made channel called the Gut, he later moved his operations to Topsham where it was easier to launch into the river. His many ships included

---

6 Swete, J. (2000). *Travels in Georgian Devon: The illustrated journals of Reverend John Swete*, Vol IV, p.166. Eds T. Gray and M. Rowe. Devon Books.

Robert Davy plaque, Topsham Church (Photo by Auguster Irabor)

naval ships for the government during the Napoleonic Wars and West Indiamen; the latter were designed to ply the Atlantic taking supplies to the plantations on the islands of the West Indies and to return with cargoes of slave-grown agricultural produce such as sugar, rum, coffee and indigo. Several of his ships were part-owned by London West India merchants leading one to question whether they played any part in the slave trade, that is, the transport of captured Africans across the Atlantic to the islands of the West Indies. The answer to this is not known.

One notable ship of Robert's is recorded in a sad 1817 memorandum by his son Daniel Bishop Davy: *"Ship called Jamaica Planter of 424 58/94 [tons] built by Robert Davy before I begun, but answered*

Site of Davy shipbuilding on Glasshouse Lane (Photo by author)

extremely well and was a very beautiful ship. ... is now lost with all hands, supposed to have foundered at sea or upset by shifting, her cargo not being properly shipped"[7] . This confirms that his ships traded with Jamaica, illustrates the great size of the ships built in the Davy shipyards, and shows the long history of ships called the Jamaica Planter (For example, another Jamaica Planter was built in Glasgow in 1959 to transport bananas from Jamaica).

The Davy shipyards were carried on at Passage in Topsham by Robert's sons, Daniel Bishop Davy and Francis Davy, until they were sold on to John Holman in 1842. The Davy shipbuilding enterprises helped to make Topsham a thriving town in the early nineteenth century.

---

7 Ponsford p.2

From top:
Waring Bowen House, Countess Wear;
Davy descendants at Waring Bowen House;
Davy dock at Passage
(All photos by author)

PART 2 SETTING UP PLANTATIONS IN JAMAICA

To Jamaica

Robert Davy had four brothers and three sisters, several of whom went to Jamaica. It is likely that they were assisted in this venture by Robert's West Indiamen ships. For example, the Exeter Flying Post of 7 March 1799 advertised: *"For Kingston Jamaica, now lying at Topsham, the good ship Grace burthen 300 tons. An entire new vessel…is neatly fitted up for the convenience of passengers, will sail the next convoy in March…For freight, passage and other particulars, apply to…Mr Robert Davy, Topsham. N.B. A respectable person is going out in the above vessel to settle at Jamaica."* It seems likely that this 'respectable person' was one of Robert's siblings, either Joan, James, John or Edward, all of whom went to Jamaica. See Davy Family Tree 1 in the Appendix.

When did the Davys first go to Jamaica? Evidence for the earliest date that Robert's brother, James Davy (1765-1825), was on the island is a deed of sale kept in the Jamaican Island Record Office that verifies the sale, on 14 January 1792, of a *"negro man slave named Prince"* from William Copland to John Davie (sic) for the sum of £100 Jamaican currency[8]. This is given in the Appendix and provides solid evidence that James Davy was an enslaver. £100 was a vast sum in those days! For comparison, the average annual wage of a full time male British agricultural labourer in the 1790s was in the region of £25[9] meaning that Davy paid an amount equal to four years' wages for Prince. A further document from the Island Record Office dated 16 July 1794 is a deed of sale of a *"negro man*

---

8 Jamaican Island Record Office (IRO) Deed. Libers, 397, folio 17.

9 Williamson, J.G., (1982). The structure of pay in Britain 1710 - 1911, *Research in Economic History*, 7.

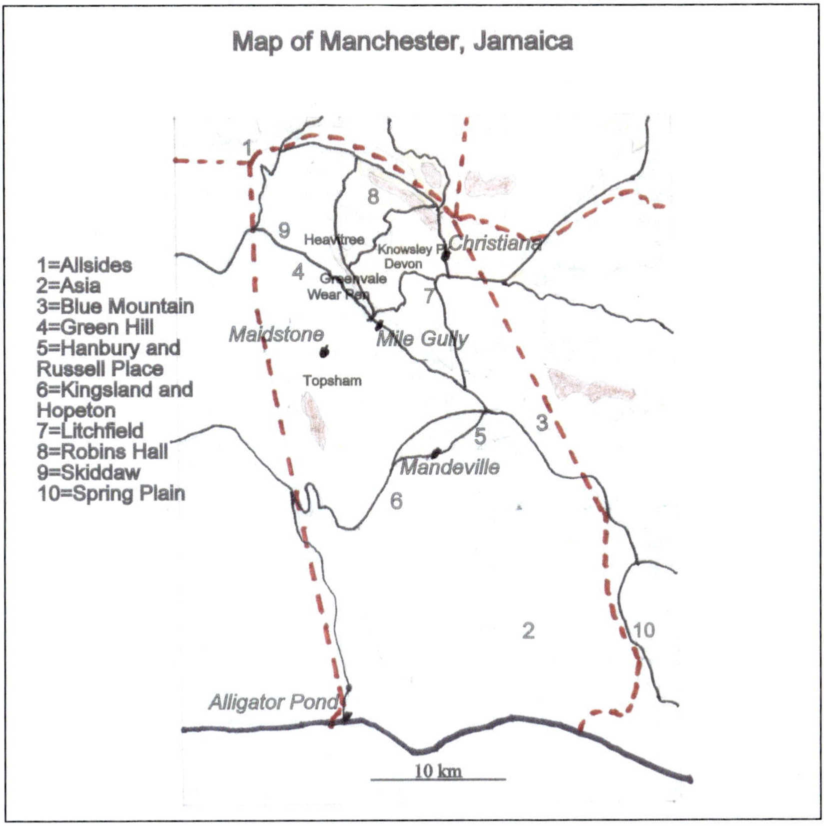

Map of Manchester, Jamaica (by author)

slave named Thomas" for £50 from Isaac Blight to James Davy[10]. It seems, therefore, that not only were they in Jamaica from the early 1790s but they were already involved in establishing plantations and purchasing enslaved Africans.

What part of Jamaica did they settle in? James is recorded in the Jamaica Almanacs[11] as owner of properties in the hilly interior of

---

10 IRO Deed 424, folio 217.

11 Available on the jamaicanfamilysearch.com website

Jamaica, called Wear Pen and Heavitree, while his brother Edward is owner of nearby Topsham. At the time these were in the parish of St Elizabeth but in 1814 they became part of the newly formed parish of Manchester. Wear Pen is near to the present-day town of Mile Gully; Heavitree is further inland from Wear Pen, while Topsham is to the south near to Maidstone.

Who named their properties? When James and Edward arrived in the 1790s, Weir Pen and Topsham already existed. They were on a map of 1764[12], shown as owned by John King and John Griffith respectively. It appears that there had been an earlier settler from Devon who had named the Topsham property. It is not known whether Wear Pen was named for Countess Wear or possibly for a previous owner with the surname Weir. The spellings are different but even today there are different opinions on the spelling of Countess Wear/ Weir. Originally I had assumed that the names had been given by these Davy men but it turned out I had jumped to a false conclusion. Heavitree was most likely named later by James Davy when he acquired this extra land higher in the hills, as it first appears in the Almanacs in 1840.

Geography of the area The scenery of this area of Jamaica is rolling wooded hills and pastured valleys which must surely have reminded the Davys of their Devon home. The main difference was the limestone geology (unlike Devon red sandstone) which means that there is a lack of rivers or surface water due to its porous nature meaning that planters would have had to set up impervious water catchments to prevent the precious rainwater from seeping away. The area was not suitable for large scale sugar cultivation because of its steep hillsides, high elevation (at over 700 metres) and therefore cooler temperatures than the prime sugar lands around the coastal plains. Instead, the land was used to raise livestock to service the

---

12 Institute of Jamaica, 15N, 4576, M300.

Heavitree Church sign (Photo by friend of author)

View of Heavitree, Jamaica (Photo by friend of author)

sugar plantations as draught animals (only a little for beef for the planters), and for coffee and pimento (allspice) for export to Britain.

Why at this particular time? The Davys' settlement in the interior hills, in what later became the parish of Manchester, was part of the 1790s coffee expansion after the 1783 reduction in British import duty[13]. It was also connected with the Haitian Revolution, a series of conflicts from 1791 to 1804 in which the victory of the formerly enslaved saw the collapse of coffee production in Jamaica's neighbouring island of Saint Domingue, and a rise in international coffee prices, making coffee a more worthwhile export crop for Jamaica, not to mention the arrival in Jamaica of French coffee planters with their expertise to share. Another factor was the defeat of the Maroons after the Second Maroon War of 1795-6, after which the Maroons – groups of Africans who had escaped their enslavement and hidden out in the hills and occasionally went on raids – were no longer a danger to white planters.

Purchase of enslaved labour This brings us to the central point of this book, that the Davys of Countess Wear were slave-owners. Having crossed the Atlantic in their brother's ship and purchased land they needed the labour to work it. This could not be provided by the indigenous Tainoo, who had been virtually exterminated by the Spanish in the sixteenth century, or by white British or Irish labourers, who had been tested in the early days of British settlement of Jamaica in the seventeenth century and found wanting due to their susceptibility to tropical diseases. Planters had found that their most profitable course of action was to import enslaved Africans and work them very hard for a few years, then replace them. The Davy brothers therefore set about purchasing Africans in large numbers for their Wear Pen and Topsham estates, in addition to Prince and Thomas mentioned above.

---

13 Higman, B.W. (1976). *Slave population and economy of Jamaica 1807-1834.* Cambridge: CUP.

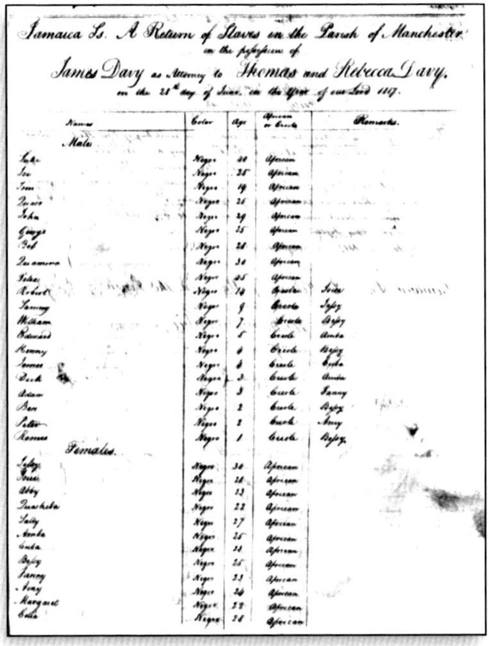

Jamaica Ss. A Return of Slaves in the Parish of Manchester in the possession of James Davy as Attorney to Thomas and Rebecca Davy, on the 28th day of June, in the Year of our Lord 1817.

Names	Color	Age	African or Creole	Remarks
Males				
Luke	Negro	40	African	
Joe	Negro	25	African	
Tom	Negro	19	African	
Quaco	Negro	26	African	
John	Negro	29	African	
George	Negro	25	African	
Bob	Negro	28	African	
Quamina	Negro	30	African	
Peter	Negro	25	African	
Robert	Negro	14	[illegible]	Joice
Sammy	Negro	9	Creole	Jessy
William	Negro	7	Creole	Betsy
Edward	Negro	5	Creole	Amba
Kenny	Negro	4	Creole	Betsy
James	Negro	4	Creole	Cuba
Dick	Negro	3	Creole	Amba
Adam	Negro	3	Creole	Fanny
Ben	Negro	2	Creole	Betsy
Peter	Negro	2	Creole	Amy
Romeo	Negro	1	Creole	Betsy
Females				
Jessy	Negro	30	African	
Joice	Negro	28	African	
Abby	Negro	33	African	
Quasheba	Negro	22	African	
Sally	Negro	27	African	
Amba	Negro	25	African	
Cuba	Negro	31	African	
Betsy	Negro	25	African	
Fanny	Negro	23	African	
Amy	Negro	24	African	
Margaret	Negro	22	African	
Celia	Negro	28	African	

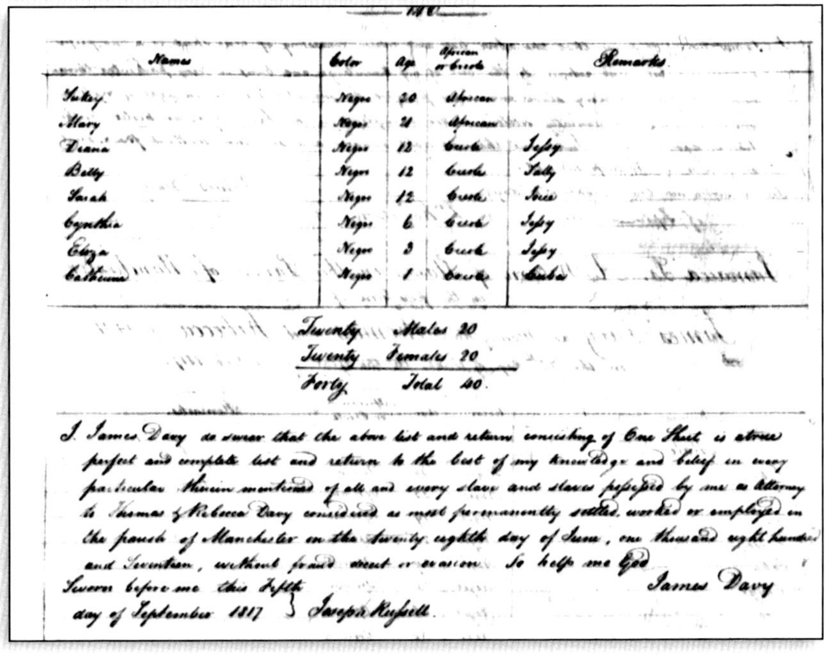

Names	Color	Age	African or Creole	Remarks
Sukey	Negro	20	African	
Mary	Negro	21	African	
Diana	Negro	12	Creole	Jessy
Betty	Negro	12	Creole	Sally
Sarah	Negro	12	Creole	Joice
Cynthia	Negro	6	Creole	Jessy
Eliza	Negro	3	Creole	Jessy
Catherine	Negro	1	Creole	Cuba

Twenty Males 20
Twenty Females 20
Forty Total 40

I James Davy do swear that the above list and return consisting of One Sheet is a true perfect and complete list and return to the best of my knowledge and belief in every particular therein mentioned of all and every slave and slaves possessed by me as Attorney to Thomas & Rebecca Davy considered as most permanently settled, worked or employed in the parish of Manchester on the twenty eighth day of June, one thousand eight hundred and Seventeen, without fraud deceit or evasion. So help me God

James Davy

Sworn before me this Fifth day of September 1817 } Joseph Russell.

Topsham Slave Register 1817 (National Archives, Kew; obtained from Ancestry.com)

An estimate of the date when the Davy brothers bought the bulk of their Africans can be obtained from the 1817 to 1833 Slave Registers[14] on which demographic information about the people held in bondage by each owner in the British West Indies had to be recorded. (See explanation of Slave Registers later).

This 1817 register for the Topsham estate shows the birthplaces of the enslaved people, either 'African' (born in Africa) or 'Creole' (born in Jamaica). The youngest African is Tom aged 19 and the oldest Creole is Robert aged 14; this gives an estimate of 1798 – 1803 for when Edward purchased them. The Africans had endured and survived capture in Africa, the journey to the coast, the horrors of the middle passage, the trauma of the slave auction on the quayside at Port Royal and then the further march in their weakened state across Jamaica to the Davy estates. This was followed by a period of 'seasoning' during which the new arrivals were accustomed to their new situation of hard labour, which they would not have experienced in their African homeland. One wonders how the infant Tom and his mother would have managed to live through these experiences.

A group of newly purchased Africans being marched from the quayside up into the hills was met at about this time by Lady Nugent[15], wife of the Governor of Jamaica. Her diary of her four years in Jamaica records: *"We met a gang of Eboe Negroes, just landed and marching up the country. I ordered the postilions to stop that I might examine their countenances as they passed, and if they looked unhappy; but they appeared perfectly the reverse. I bowed, kissed my hand, and laughed; they did the same. The women, in particular seemed pleased, and all admired the carriage &c"*. The Igbo (Eboe) were an

---

14 Former British Colonial Dependencies, Slave Register, 1813-1834; available on Ancestry.com

15 Nugent, M. (1839). *A journal of a voyage to, and residence in, the island of Jamaica from 1801 to 1805*. London.

African people living to the east of the Niger River in the Bight of Biafra, an area heavily resourced by British slave traders in the late eighteenth century[16]. Had they been bought by the Davy brothers? The Davys may have been to the slave market on the quay at Port Royal and bought a number of Igbo people and then marched them the eighty miles across the island up to their properties in the hills. They seem to have had a lively sense of humour!

Topsham and Edward Davy

Topsham in Jamaica was settled by Edward Davy. The Jamaica Almanacs show that it was a property of 280 acres growing coffee and pimento. The earliest Almanac shows that it had 31 enslaved workers in 1811 which had grown to 48 by 1826. Unfortunately, Edward did not live long and in his will of 1804[17] he left the bulk of his property – that is, his land and enslaved people – to be shared by his brother Dr Thomas Davy of Ottery St Mary (England) and sister Rebecca of Countess Wear (England), who would become absentee slave-owners. Topsham would then be managed by their brother James Davy as 'attorney'[18].

The Church of England baptism records in Jamaica show the baptism of Edward's common-law wife Elizabeth Morgan, a free mulatto aged 17, and their baby daughter Jane Davy aged 3 months, in 1802[19]. Sadly, Edward was soon writing his will, in which he left some of his assets *"unto Elizabeth Morgan, a free mulatto woman whom I now keep"*; these included some money,

---

16 The Transatlantic Slave Trade Database at *https://www.slavevoyages.org/voyage/database* accessed Feb 2021.

17 Island Record Office, Manchester Wills, Vol 73.

18 An attorney in this context is the person appointed to act for the absentee owner. It does not imply that they were legally qualified.

19 Jamaica, Church of England Parish Register Transcripts, 1664-1880 St Elizabeth > Baptisms, marriages, burials 1705-1820>image 55 of 180; Registrar General's Department, Spanish Town.

View of Topsham, Jamaica (Photo by friend of author)

25 acres of woodland, and three negro women. Thus Elizabeth, a woman of mixed race who was not enslaved (because she was 'free'), was given three black women to be her domestic 'slaves'. To their baby daughter, Jane, he left £1000, *"to be sent to England at the age of eight years to have a decent education"*. One wonders whether Jane ever came to England, and, if she did, which of her relatives she stayed with. It is interesting to think that a mixed-race girl may have been living in Countess Wear two hundred years ago!

Another young man from Topsham (England) arrived at Topsham (Jamaica) in 1807. This was 23 year-old Christopher Ramson whose father was a basket-maker and thatcher who gathered his reeds from a plot in Newcourt, next to Countess Wear. Christopher would most probably have been employed as a 'book-keeper' on the estate, a role that really meant overseeing the forced labour of the enslaved Africans. Information passed down in his family describes

Topsham Church, Jamaica (Photo by friend of author)

Topsham as *"high in the Don Figuerero mountains, approached by a zigzag path of some 7 or 8 miles through forests of tree-ferns, palms and flowering trees such as the scarlet flowered Flame of the Forest and the mauve Jacaranda.…Firewood… was cut by slaves who did not use the winding path but went barefoot straight up the mountainside"*[20]. This illustrates the marked contrast between the beauty of the tropical island and the harshness of its history of enslavement.

After the death of James Davy in 1825 the management of Topsham passed to a succession of other attorneys. It is not clear when it was sold. Topsham was closely associated with Knowsley Park estate, seven miles away, also owned by the Davy family, which stayed within the family until at least the 1850s.

---

20 Coombes, I., TOPMS: PH38.22 Estuary Magazine, July 1976.

Wear Pen and James Davy

Wear Pen was settled by James Davy. The Jamaica Almanacs show that Wear Pen and the associated Heavy Tree together occupied 1724 acres in 1839 and, unlike Topsham, it was primarily a ranch for rearing stock – hence the name 'pen'. The terrain at Wear Pen was less steep than Topsham and hence more suitable for raising cattle, horses and mules. It is still surrounded by lush green fields, good for cattle; James had no doubt learned a lot about cattle farming in his childhood on Wear Barton Farm back home in Devon. At its peak in 1821 it had 399 stock. The oxen were raised to do the heavy work on sugar estates, turning the machinery to grind the sugar cane and pulling the heavy cane carts from the fields to the factories. As described earlier, Heavitree would have focussed on coffee production as the land was further into the mountains and a lot steeper.

Remains of Wear Pen House 2007
(Photo by friend of author)

Above: *Wear Pen Church with Geoffrey and Primrose Davy 2011*
(Photo by author)

Left: *Wear Pen churchyard*
(Photo by author)

James married a white woman, Hannah Aslin, in St Elizabeth (Jamaica) in 1794, and the marriage produced four daughters and three sons. The first three children were born in St Elizabeth, Jamaica (Mary Elizabeth 1796; Anne Maria 1798; James Lewis 1799) and all baptised together there in 1800[21] while the others were born in England - John was born 1801 at Heydon Cottage, Topsham, and baptised in Exminster (1801), while the last three children, George Thomas (born Topsham 1803), Frances Portbury (born 1805) and Eliza Powell[22] (born 1806), were baptised together in Alphington in 1808. They were recorded as living in Exminster at the time. The two who are of most interest here are James Lewis (1799-1840) and John (1800-1863). See Family Tree 2 in Appendix.

The naming of the second son James Lewis is interesting – does it relate to a possible romantic interest between the father and Mary Ann Lewis, spinster of St Elizabeth, in whose 1808 will she stipulates: *'It is my wish that my Executors do have a ring made of my hair the value of two Guineas and present unto Mr. James Davy like token of Remembrance*[23]?

It is unclear where James Davy was actually living at this time as he seemed to be frequently travelling back and forth between Devon and Jamaica. He was having children in Exminster (Devon) but also, in the Jamaican records for St Elizabeth, he is recorded as being a justice of the peace in 1801 and witnessing the above will in 1808. We know he returned to Jamaica in 1813 because it was stated in his father's 1813 will that James was "*now on his passage to Jamaica*". We know he was in Jamaica in 1817 and 1820 because

21 Jamaica Church of England Parish Register Transcripts 1664 – 1880, St. Elizabeth. Available on FamilySearch.

22 England, Devon Bishop's Transcripts 1558-1887. Accessed on FamilySearch.

23 Families from Anglican Parish Registers and Wills, Descendants of George Ruggles, accessed on jamaicanfamilysearch.com.

we can view his signature on the Slave Registers. It is surprising how often these people made the long and hazardous Atlantic crossing between Devon and their Jamaican properties! Living in Exminster, the children would have been only a mile away from their grandfather James (1729-1813), aunt Rebecca (1759-1827) and uncle Robert the shipbuilder (1762-1862) in Countess Wear. Perhaps they played with their cousins, Robert's children, who would later take over his shipbuilding and other businesses, and build two notable houses in Topsham, Devon: Daniel Bishop Davy built Grove Hill House and Francis Davy built Riversmeet House. Did the family return to Jamaica with their father in 1813? It is likely that his sons remained at school in England, as they would have been aged 14, 12 and 10 at this time. We know that his eldest son, at least, was highly educated as he became Dr James Lewis Davy M.D.

James cultivated Wear Pen until his son John took over in 1823,

James Davy tomb at Clyst St Mary Church, Devon (Photo by author)

shortly before his father's death in 1825. James' tombstone is back in Devon, in the churchyard of Clyst St Mary. James' will leaves a substantial sum to his family - £3000[24] each to the four daughters and youngest son, George, plus £1000 to his wife, Hannah, 'to enable her to settle herself in England' as well as an annuity of £500. The rest of his property was to be shared by James Lewis and John as tenants in common[25].

John Davy plaque, Wear Pen Church, Jamaica (Photo by friend of author)

John remained in charge of Wear Pen and Heavitree for many years after slavery was abolished, finally returning to England in 1860. He was commemorated in Jamaica by a plaque in St George's church near to Wear Pen. John has many descendants – further details about them will be discussed at a later point.

Agricultural economy in the hills of Jamaica 1790s to 1830s

The following is taken from Higman[26] and Shepherd[27].

The Davy properties in the hills of central Jamaica grew coffee and pimento for export and raised livestock on 'pens' mainly as

---

24 Worth about £240,000 in today's money

25 IRO Wills, Manchester, Vol 106, p.138.

26 Higman, B.W. (1988). *Jamaica surveyed: Plantation maps and plans of the nineteenth century.* Kingston: Institute of Jamaica Publications.

27 Shepherd, V. (1991). Trade and exchange in Jamaica in the period of slavery. In H. Beckles and V. Shepherd (eds) *Caribbean slave society and economy.* Kingston: Ian Randle.

working animals for the sugar estates on the lower land around the coasts. These plantations and pens were less capital-intensive than sugar estates and required less labour. The most efficient size of a sugar estate required around 200 workers, factory buildings for the processing of the sugar cane into a crystalline form for export, and distillation facilities for making rum and, while coffee also required some processing (washing, drying, husking), it was less than for sugar, and there were fewer agricultural tasks. Thus the capital outlay for these upland planters like the Davys was less than for the longer established sugar estates on the prime lowland areas, but the potential profits were also more modest. This meant that owners of coffee plantations and pens were less likely to be able to retire to the comfort of Britain and more likely to be resident on their Jamaican property. By the 1830s, 80% of Jamaican sugar estates were owned by absentees while it was the other way round for coffee (25% absentees) and pens (15% absentees). In our Davy family, Topsham (Jamaica) became owned by absentees after Edward's 1803 death (Dr Thomas and sister Rebecca) while Wear Pen was owned by the (occasional) resident James, which was more typical.

The fact that the livestock on the pens were destined for the sugar estates meant that the pens were not independent units (unlike the coffee and pimento plantations) but had significant links with the sugar estates. The latter needed a large number of new working stock each year, even 100 new working steers, at high prices (e.g. the 1820 price of a mule was £40, equivalent to about £3,000 in today's money). Cattle were more suitable than horses as draught animals; horses were used for riding and were more expensive to buy and maintain. It was the job of some enslaved workers to drive the stock from the pens to the sugar estates and this gave them a greater freedom of mobility than enjoyed by the majority of enslaved people.

How were the coffee and pimento exported?

It is likely that the Davy crops were carried to a port on the south coast for export, such as Black River, Old Harbour or Alligator Pond, which was the nearest wharf to the Davy plantations. The Jamaican Assembly in 1810 approved the construction of a road down to the wharf at Alligator Pond from central Manchester and it is interesting to note that Thomas Phillpotts (brother of Henry Phillpotts, Bishop of Exeter) was one of the trustees on this project. A toll was charged for coffee transported on this road[28].

Conditions of the enslaved workers

Slave codes

The legal basis of slavery in the British West Indies was first formulated in the 1661 Barbados Slave Code, which was exported to Jamaica with Thomas Modyford (son of a mayor of Exeter) in 1664 and adopted in this island in 1696. It subsequently went through modifications as enslaved people resisted and rebelled against their situation and the white population tried to maintain their ascendance and safety, introducing more stringent measures, and these were codified in 1781 by the Jamaican Assembly[29]. The Slave Code established the chattel status of the black slave, the continuance of slave status of children through their mother, the inferior status of blacks to whites, their subjection to the power of their master, their lack of access to justice, their liability to harsh and inhumane punishments, and restrictions on their freedom of movement. On the other hand the code did stipulate that the master provide a proper measure of food and clothing, and

---

28 *Laws of Jamaica* Vol. 6 (1817), 41. (I am indebted to Peter Wingfield-Digby for this information)

29 Smith, R.W. (1945). The legal status of Jamaican slaves before the anti-slavery movement. *The Journal of Negro History,* 30(3) pp.293-303. Accessed Feb 2021 on JStor.

prohibited extreme cruelty (in theory).

Punishments

Punishment of slaves was severe – how else could they be made to work when there was no financial or other reward? Slave drivers carried a whip – the universal symbol of slavery. As well as severe floggings for minor offences, enslaved people could be mutilated, for example by having their nose slit, or even dismembered. Being completely at the mercy of their masters, they were sometimes put to death in a barbarous fashion, by being burnt alive or left to die of hunger and thirst in a cage. The Diaries of Thomas Thistlewood[30] detail his treatment of enslaved people during his work as overseer on a Jamaican estate, giving the lead slave driver 300 lashes for negligence, and over eleven months whipping more than half of the enslaved people, giving at least 50 lashes each time. By the early nineteenth century, the treadmill was commonly used, and transportation to a Spanish island became a more favoured way for a planter to get rid of a troublesome slave.

Skull Point

A local example of this brutality was at the place now named Skull Point[31]. Skull point is very close to the Davy property at Wear Pen. It is so named because it is said that the skull of an enslaved man called James Knight was stuck on a post here and displayed as a warning to others. His crime was to have become converted to Christianity and then preaching to his fellow enslaved people. His owner had objected violently and had him beheaded. His spirit is said to have haunted the area ever since. He was said to be from the Lyndhurst estate, one of the properties registered to John

---

30 *Diary of Thomas Thistlewood, 1748-1786,* Monsoon 31, vols 1-37, Lincolnshire County Archives.

31 Roving with Lala, *Jamaica Gleaner*, March 19, 2009. *mobile.jamaica-gleaner.com/20090319/news/news1.php*

Davy in the 1840 Almanacs, though the beheading would have happened some years before this. I was unable to find any reference to a James Knight in the Slave Registers for Lyndhurst.

Work of the enslaved people

Skull Point sign, Mile Gully (Photo by friend of author)

The British West Indies were primarily sugar-growing islands, making enormous profits for proprietors which were fed back to the mother country and, to some extent, invested in productive enterprises feeding the success of the Industrial Revolution[32]. Many particular examples of slave-owners' commercial and physical legacies have been identified[33]. Sugar estates were monocultures on which the enslaved workers underwent long hours of heavy labour in the hot sun under close supervision and harsh discipline. Workers on plantations and pens such as Topsham and Wear also had long hours of hard work, albeit less arduous than on sugar estates. Higman[34] estimates that labourers on coffee plantations and pens worked an average of approximately 3,100 hours per year while those of sugar estates worked 4,000 hours per year. By comparison, a British factory worker in the 1830s

---

32 Williams, E.E. (1964). *Capitalism and slavery.* London: Andre Deutsch.

33 www.ucl.ac.uk/lbs/legacies

34 Higman, B.W. (1984). *Slave populations of the British Caribbean 1807-1834.* Baltimore: Johns Hopkins.

would have worked 2,900 hours and a modern worker 2,000 hours annually. In terms of hours worked, the enslaved workers on the Davy plantations were somewhat better off than their compatriots on the lowland cane fields but less well off than British workers in the newly industrialised workplaces (who were at least paid for their work).

Specific jobs done on the three types of plantation

Each type of agriculture on the Davys' plantations had its own tasks to be carried out. On each type of plantation the enslaved workers were divided into three gangs based on physical strength and given tasks accordingly. In addition, there were specialised roles such as carpenter and seamstress, as well as positions of some power such as (slave) driver. Women were as likely as men to be doing heavy manual work.

Livestock pens. With livestock, the strongest workers, the 'great gang' did jobs such as cutting down trees and mending fences; the second gang, of the older adults and teenagers, performed lighter tasks such as weeding and shelling corn; while the small gang (i.e. the children above the age of about six) had jobs like carrying grass to the stables. There were also grooms and stockmen. Work on the pens was less regimented than on a sugar plantation, with more individual tasks allowing greater independence. In this way it was harder for the whites to control their enslaved workers than in the closely supervised labour system on the sugar plantations but this was offset by the smaller size of the community and the greater closeness to the master which limited freedom in other ways[35].

Coffee planting necessitated felling the original trees and burning the brushwood, then digging holes to plant the young coffee trees; subsequently the annual jobs consisted of weeding and pruning

---

35 Higman, B.W. (1976). Slave population and economy in Jamaica 1807-1834. Cambridge: CUP.

Pimento trees at Topsham (Photo by friend of author)

Drying pimento berries (Photo by author)

the young trees, and at harvest time picking the berries and drying them on a flat area called a barbecue.

Pimento, also called Jamaican allspice, was valued as a spice said to combine the flavours of cinnamon, nutmeg and cloves. It is made from drying the unripe berries of the tree, producing hard brown berries that resemble peppercorns. The tall pimento trees were grown in conjunction with coffee bushes to provide the needed shade. Production was less labour-intensive than coffee and jobs were allocated on a task basis.

These, then, were the businesses that James and Edward Davy had established at Wear Pen, Topsham and Heavitree, and the tasks they had to organise, getting their enslaved workers to carry out the labour.

Food of the enslaved people

Responsibility for feeding the plantation population was shared between the master and his enslaved people. Each plantation had its own provision ground where enslaved workers grew their own crops. These consisted of starchy roots such as yams, dasheens and cocoyams; other staple crops like breadfruit, plantains and corn (maize); and varieties of legumes such as gungo peas and red kidney beans. Fruit trees, like mango and ackee, and coconut palms completed the smallholdings. From these grounds enslaved people were expected to feed themselves to a greater or lesser extent, using their Sunday – their only day off – for this work. The slave-owner was expected to provide their protein in the form of salted cod which would have been imported from the Newfoundland banks[36], as well as flour and corn imported from North America. Food shortages arose when the provision grounds were damaged by drought or hurricane, and when imports to the island were reduced in times of war (e.g. War between Britain and America 1812-1815). These resulted in great hardships for enslaved people including malnutrition and near starvation.

---

36 Devon ports such as Teignmouth and Barnstaple were active in the Newfoundland fisheries.

PART 3 AFRICANS ENSLAVED BY THE DAVYS

Background to the Slave Registers

Abolition Movement

During these same years that James and Edward were getting established as slave-owners, an increasing repugnance against slavery and the slave trade was spreading in Britain, with the Society for the Abolition of the Slave Trade being formed in 1787. In 1788, for example, following Thomas Clarkson's visit to Exeter, a list of more than 250 local contributors to the Society was drawn up and, in 1792, meetings were held such as that at the Salutation Inn in Topsham, Devon, at which an Abolition petition was signed by many Topsham people[37]. The thinking behind the campaign – which was only aimed at abolishing the **trade** in human beings, not the institution of slavery itself - was that West Indian planters would be forced to treat their enslaved workers more humanely if their supply of fresh Africans through the slave trade was eliminated. The reason for the continuation of the slave trade despite the huge numbers of Africans already transported to the West Indies had been that their numbers on plantations were continually falling due to their high mortality rate and low birth rate as a result of the harsh treatment they endured. Therefore cutting off the supply of fresh Africans was expected to lead to planters being forced to improve conditions in their own interest. After a long campaign, fought against the entrenched interests of the planter class represented in Parliament by MPs of the West India Interest (such as Charles Rose

37 Di Cooper, 2021. Exeter-Abolitionists-DC.pdf (tellingourstoriesdevon.org.uk)

Ellis[38]), the Act for the Abolition of the Slave Trade was eventually passed in 1807.

Amelioration and the Slave Registers

The expected outcome did not, however, occur and deaths continued to exceed births on sugar plantations. This led to further public pressure on the British Government to enforce formal 'Amelioration' measures on the West Indian planters, such as prohibiting the flogging of women, prohibiting the breaking up of enslaved families by sale, limiting hours of work, introducing instruction in the Christian religion and the right of the enslaved to own property. Some monitoring of the success of Amelioration was to be achieved by the keeping of Slave Registers which would particularly record numbers of enslaved people for each owner and account for increases and decreases on a three-yearly basis. Registers would also reveal illegal slave trading. These Slave Registers are now a source of valuable information for the researcher yielding insights into the lives and deaths of the enslaved people which would not otherwise have been recorded. Throughout this book I have made extensive use of the Slave Registers to investigate the histories of the enslaved people, as a group and as individuals, on the Davy plantations.

It should be borne in mind that the registers have limitations. They have been criticised by Carby[39] as being essentially lists of property, which therefore degrade the humanity of the people on the lists. They lack accuracy (ages of 'slaves' were approximate guesses); they are in the name of the owner not the property (which could lead

---

38 Head of the West India Interest for many years and associated with Mamhead House, Dawlish. See Taylor, M. (2020). *The Interest: How the British establishment resisted the abolition of slavery*. London: Bodley Head.

39 Carby, H.V. (2019). *Imperial intimacies: A tale of two islands*. London: Verso.

to confusion when the same person had several properties in the same parish), and there is the possibility of cheating because the lists were verified by other slave-owners in the same social milieu. Nevertheless, Higman's thorough analyses of the Slave Registers did not lead him to believe that they were widely different from the reality of the demographic situation.

Davy Slave Registers

In this section I will look at what the Slave Registers for Topsham and Wear Pen tell us about the names, status and religion of the enslaved people, their births and deaths, places of birth, motherhood and family size, racial categories, manumission and resistance to bondage.

Names, status and religion

The naming of the enslaved people tells a fascinating story of their change in status in Jamaican society. Before the Slave Registers, the Jamaican Almanacs (available on jamaicanfamilysearch.com) from as early as 1811 listed the Davy properties with their owners, 'slaves' and stock:

> *Davy, James, Wear 75 / 256*
> *Davy, Thomas, Topsham 31 / 8*

The first figure is the number of enslaved people and the second the number of stock. This illustrates that enslaved people and stock

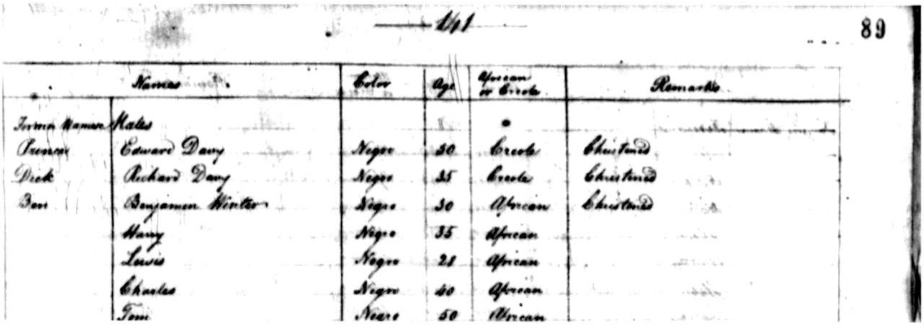

141 89

Former Names	Names	Color	Age	African or Creole	Remarks
	Males				
Prince	Edward Davy	Negro	50	Creole	Christened
Dick	Richard Davy	Negro	35	Creole	Christened
Ben	Benjamin Winter	Negro	30	African	Christened
	Harry	Negro	35	African	
	Lewis	Negro	21	African	
	Charles	Negro	40	African	
	Tom	Negro	50	African	

Extract from 1817 Topsham Slave Register showing that some men had surnames (National Archives, Kew; obtained from Ancestry.com)

were given a similar status in pre-emancipation[40] Jamaica. These African people were not given full human status. In the 1817 Slave Registers, enslaved people had just one name, often somewhat ridiculous, as would be given to a dog or a cow. The captured Africans had been stripped of their own names, along with as much of their identity and culture as their white captors had been able to remove, and given new names to reflect their new lowly status. Thus in Wear Pen we find Devonshire, Topsham and Fortune, and in the Topsham estate there are Topsy and Queen.

There are exceptions to this, however. At Wear Pen, three older men are listed as having former names and new names. Prince, whose purchase was mentioned earlier, is now at the age of 50 called Edward Davy; this is explained by his having been christened. These new names consist of a Christian name and a surname, and demonstrate a rise in status. These three must have been the senior men with responsibilities; probably they were slave drivers whose job was to force the others to work and who carried a whip to ensure obedience.

---

40 In Britain, 'abolition' is used in the 'abolition of the slave trade' and the 'abolition of slavery'. In the Caribbean, 'emancipation' is used instead of the 'abolition of slavery'. Here I prefer the Caribbean usage.

Other exceptions are quite different – they are children. There are seven girls and two boys under the age of 15 at Wear Pen who have been christened – the reason is that their mothers were senior women who, like Prince, had been christened. The youngest is Isabella Davy aged two, whose former name was Thisbe; her mother was a 32 year old African now called Ruth Davy but formerly known as Alice. It is likely that these mothers were 'house slaves' in contrast to the majority who were 'field slaves'. House slaves were domestic workers in the plantation house who tended to the intimate needs of the master's family and who thereby became quite close to the whites.

The important thing here is that being a Christian was seen as having fully human status and being undeniably above the condition of animals. It did not necessarily entail any religious conversion. Part of the programme of Amelioration being pressed upon the Jamaican planters by the government in London was that enslaved people should be taught to be more 'civilised' and a key aspect of this was to be taught the Christian religion. The planters and their representatives in the Jamaican Assembly were against this, as was the Anglican Church, so efforts in this direction were mainly nominal. Any real attempts to teach the enslaved were made by the non-conformists, often in the teeth of opposition from the establishment. Thus Baptists and Moravians were active as missionaries and as campaigners for emancipation and for improving the lot of enslaved people. The Anglican church of St George's, built next to the Wear Pen property on land donated by the Davys, was intended for the white elite of the area, not for the enslaved masses.

Records of baptism found in the Jamaican Island Records Office show that, on 10th March 1820, the Topsham property had 26 of their enslaved people baptised, while on the same day at Wear

Pen 103 were baptised[41]. This appeared to be an empty ritual with the aim of satisfying the law. But this presents a problem to the researcher who is trying to trace names across the Registers as most of the names listed in the 1832 Wear Pen Register are quite different from those in the 1817 Register, apart from those few already mentioned who were christened at an earlier date. It is only the 1820 baptism records held at the Island Record Office that has both the new and former names. Nevertheless, this would be enough information for a descendant to trace their ancestry back to an enslaved person.

This process did give the enslaved people a freedom that most of us don't get, and that is to choose our own name, both given name and surname[42]. The 1832 Wear Pen Register shows that Davy was the most popular choice of surname, while other choices were Williams, Dixon, Wilson, Vassall, and many others. It was the most usual custom for enslaved people to take the surname of their owner though this was by no means compulsory, and the other surnames would have been taken from other white people known by the enslaved, people who worked as overseers, book-keepers and attorneys on the estates. This is why Jamaicans today have these British surnames. These surnames provide clues as to the estates on which their ancestors were enslaved.

Births and deaths

A study of the Slave Registers for Topsham and Wear Pen allows us to learn about births and deaths on these plantations because these had to be reported every three years, with names and ages, as part of the programme of Amelioration explained above. Over the whole

---

41 IRO Manchester Register Vol 1, p.139

42 Burton, R.D.E. (1999). Names and naming in Afro-Caribbean cultures. *New West Indian Guide 73, 1*. p. 40. Though it is not clear to what extent the enslaved people did have freedom of choice.

fifteen year period from 1817 to 1832 their combined number of reported births was 58 and of deaths was 32; births therefore outstripped deaths by 26, allowing a slow growth in numbers. This contrasted with the situation on the sugar plantations where deaths exceeded births, indicating that working conditions on the coffee plantations and cattle pens were not as harsh as on the sugar plantations.

Births of enslaved children at Topsham and Wear Pen 1817-1832

The number of births reported in the Slave Registers are shown in this table. It should be noted that not all births were reported due to the high rate of infant mortality, so book-keepers tended to wait until the child had lived beyond the first few months. The table indicates an irregularly increasing trend, with slightly more male than female births.

Births of enslaved children from Slave Registers

Year	Topsham males	Topsham females	Wear Pen males	Wear Pen females	Total
1817-1819	2	0	2	2	6
1820-1822	4	4	3	2	13
1823-1825	3	1	4	1	9
1826-1828	4	4	3	3	14
1829-1832	1	3	6	6	16
Total	**14**	**12**	**18**	**14**	**58**

With the same caveat, that deaths of infants were not consistently reported, the number of deaths on the two estates is shown below. It indicates a fairly steady rate of deaths, with somewhat more female than male deaths.

Deaths of enslaved people at Topsham and Wear Pen

Year	Topsham males	Topsham females	Wear Pen males	Wear Pen females	Total
1817-1819	0	3	2	3	8
1820-1822	1	0	2	1	4
1823-1825	0	1	3	2	6
1826-1828	1	1	1	2	5
1829-1832	1	1	3	4	9
Total	**3**	**6**	**11**	**12**	**32**

How long did they live?

The Registers give the (approximate) ages of death, as shown in this table.

Ages of death by gender on Topsham and Wear Pen 1817 to 1832

Age at death (years)	Males	Females	Total
0-9	2	3	5
10-19	1	2	3
20-29	3	2	5
30-39	4	7	11
40-49	3	3	6
50-59	0	1	1
60-69	1	0	1
Total	**14**	**18**	**32**

Despite certain inconsistencies in the registers, it is clear that deaths of both males and females reached a peak in their thirties. This may be attributed to their harsh living and working conditions, overwork and poor nutrition, and the hazards of childbirth. What this table under-reports is the rate of infant mortality, as explained above. Also it does not show that, in fact, a large proportion of the enslaved did live beyond their thirties despite the harsh conditions; they had not yet reached old age during the time of the Registers. This pattern of births and deaths resulted in a change in the age structure of the enslaved population over the period.

Age Structure

The following chart shows the age structure of the Wear Pen enslaved population at two points in time: in 1817 when the original Slave Register was drawn up and then in 1832 when a new register happened to be made following the death of James Davy and the inheritance of Wear Pen by his two eldest sons, John Davy and James Lewis Davy. It illustrates that, while the numbers had grown, the number of enslaved people in the prime working age group (15-39 years) had actually shrunk. The increase was due to the survival of many into the 40+ age group where they would have

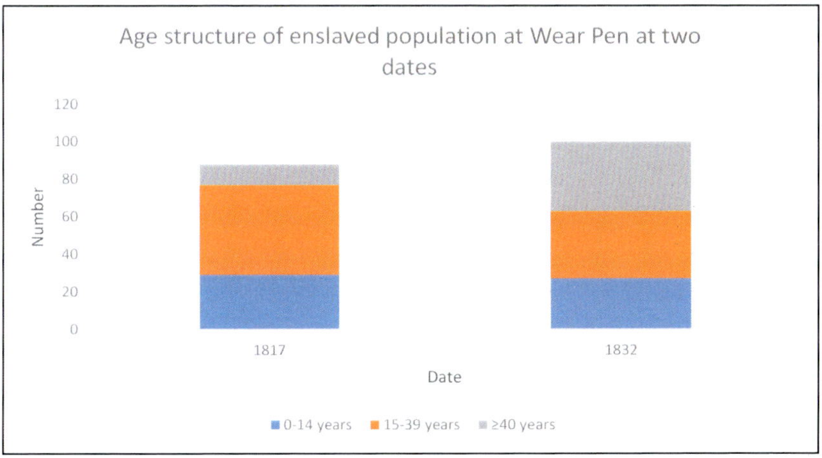

been less efficient from the Davy point of view but still needing to be fed and clothed. From the enslaved workers' point of view it suggests that the heavy work that had formerly been done by workers in their prime now had to be shared with the older people and teenagers – a unintended outcome of the abolition of the slave trade?

Closer examination of the figures shows that the African-born had moved up from the prime working age group (15-39 years) in 1817 to the older age group (≥40 years) by 1832 to be partially, but not completely, replaced by the next generation, born in Jamaica; and that a similar process had happened for males and females. The youngest group (0-14 years) were entirely Jamaican-born. This gap in the prime working years was common to other coffee plantations in the hills of Jamaica and may help to account for a fall in production from its 1814 peak (though soil erosion and soil exhaustion also played a part)[43]. This problem for the planter had been predicted by their representatives in the Jamaica Assembly in 1804 and used as an argument against the abolition of the slave trade. This change in the age structure would have led to a shortage of workers in the great gang, who tackled the heaviest jobs, and perhaps an excess in the second gang, who could only manage the lighter tasks.

Looking at our Davy plantations in comparison to the larger Caribbean picture, analyses of the Slave Registers carried out by Higman allowed him to discern several demographic trends which shed light on the living conditions of enslaved populations across the Caribbean. For example, estate records show that coffee plantations in Manchester were most productive and profitable in the early years of the nineteenth century, with highest production in 1814. He attributes this success to the young age of the workforce

---

43 Higman (1976).

due to their recent arrival from Africa. The Topsham slave register of 1817, for instance, shows that the oldest man, Luke, was only 40 years old and the oldest woman, Topsy, only 30. As the years went by the enslaved Africans became older and less healthy and so less productive and were more likely to die. The 1826 Slave Register for Wear Pen records that three men (Topsham, Isaac and Abraham) had died aged 36, 38 and 37, depriving James Davy of three of his workers in their prime. The Davys would have had considerable difficulty maintaining the profitability of their plantations for this reason.

Motherhood

Childlessness

Slave-owners, needing to maintain their workforce, were concerned with the fertility of their enslaved women but low fertility remained a problem despite measures taken during Amelioration to promote the health and welfare of pregnant and nursing mothers. Were these measures insufficient or was it due to deliberate actions of women refusing to have children, as the planter class contended[44]? Planters accused women of lacking a maternal instinct and carrying out abortion and infanticide. Some light was shed on this by Dunn's comparative study of a Jamaican sugar estate and a Virginian mixed agriculture slave-holding, in which he estimated that there was a far higher rate of childlessness on the Jamaican estate (at least 40%) than the Virginian one (about 10%). He was able to link this to the harsher conditions of enslavement in Jamaica in terms of disease, malnutrition and the brutality of the labour regime.

---

44 Dunn, R.S. (2014) *A tale of two plantations: Slave life and labor in Jamaica and Virginia.* Cambridge, Mass: Harvard University Press. Also *'Motherhood, childlessness, and the care of children from slavery to Emancipation'* Conference held at University of Reading 2016. Also De la Beche, H. (1825) Notes of the present conditions of the negroes in Jamaica, in *Tracts*, British Library.

I thought it would be instructive to try to extract information on childlessness from the Davy slave registers to compare with Dunn's figures. I came across the difficulty that the change of names described above, when the enslaved people were christened, meant that I could not trace the same women all the way through the series of registers, especially on Wear Pen, so I restricted my analysis to Topsham up until 1829 where the names are traceable. Ages were recorded very approximately, often guesses.

The figures are summarised in the next table, together with women (females over the age of 15 in 1829) who neither gave birth nor died (according to the Registers) so may be assumed to be childless.

Topsham mothers and their children

Mother's name	African/ Creole	Age at end of period 1829	Number of children recorded
Bessy	African	(died 1826 aged 33)	6
Fanny (Jane Davy)	African	35	6
Sally (Eve Davy)	African	39	5
Cuba	African	35	4
Topsy	African	42	4
Amy (Amelia Davy)	African	36	3
Sarah (Sarah Bramwell)	Creole	24	3
Joice	African	40	2
Betty	Creole	24	1
Abby	African	35	0
Celia	African	40	0

Cynthia	Creole	18	0
Diana	Creole	24	0
Margaret	African	34	0
Mary	African	33	0
Quasheba	African	(died 1829 aged 34)	0
Sukey	African	32	0
Totals 17 women	**13 African /4 Creole**		**34 children**

It appears that, out of the 17 enslaved women who had lived on the Topsham estate between 1817 and 1829, nine were mothers but eight were not. Of course, some of the childless women may have gone on to have children later, especially the two younger, Creole, women, but the other six, African, women were in their thirties or forties and had not apparently given birth up until this time and so were unlikely to do so.

This high proportion of childless women (8/17 = 47%) is in line with observations of Dunn for the Jamaican sugar plantation. Mine is likely to be an over-estimate, as explained above, and can only be illustrative due to the small sample size, but it does tend to suggest that the phenomenon of childlessness existed on the Davy plantations as it did elsewhere on the island, and therefore that conditions of labour for these women were too demanding for their bodies to be able to cope with childbirth as well.

Family size

The nine mothers produced 34 children altogether, averaging 3.8 children per mother. This compares with Dunn's figures of 2.9 children per mother for the Jamaican and 4.3 for the Virginian plantation. This makes sense as already explained that conditions were somewhat easier for Jamaican enslaved workers on a coffee plantation than on a sugar plantation. Conditions for enslaved workers in North America were a lot easier than in Jamaica; the former's population increased over the decades, soon rendering the transatlantic slave trade unnecessary. Thus an intermediate position for the Davys' coffee plantation is reasonable.

Another instructive figure to look at is the small number of women who produced most of the children on the Topsham estate. In Dunn's study, a small number of women on the sugar plantation produced most of the babies; at Topsham, the top three mothers in the above table (Bessy, Fanny and Sally) produced half of all the babies – 17 out of the 34 – as many as the other 14 women put together. Dunn comments on the remarkable ability of a few women to be fertile in the teeth of the extreme demands of their lives. It seems that Bessy, Fanny and Sally also had this toughness, that having survived the middle passage on ship from Africa as young girls, they were still fit enough to give birth to many children. Perhaps they were house slaves with a somewhat easier life than for those working in the fields. Whether they were happy with this prolific motherhood we won't ever know, but Thomas and Rebecca Davy must have been pleased to receive these valuable additions to their human property, for which they would soon be claiming compensation when Emancipation arrived.

The 'survival gene' is often spoken about in Jamaica as being something that enabled their ancestors to survive the middle passage and the brutalities of slavery, producing a strong and vibrant people today. The foregoing analysis adds weight to this idea in that some enslaved women did more than simply survive, they lived to pass on their genes to a new generation, while others lived but did not pass on their genes. This is a clear example of 'selection pressure'; Bessy, Fanny and Sally had genes that gave them a competitive advantage over others such as Abby and Celia, so that only the former were able to pass on their genes to future Jamaicans. The 'survival gene' (not a single gene but a combination of inherited traits) is sometimes blamed for the high prevalence of modern diseases such as diabetes, hypertension and obesity in Jamaica as it is proposed that a physiology that can survive deprivation and hardship by making very efficient use of scarce nutrients will easily succumb to problems of over-nutrition in times of comparative plenty.

Grandmothers

The Slave Registers enable us to reconstruct short family trees for some of the enslaved people on Topsham and Wear Pen; these encompass three generations from the African grandmother down to the Creole daughters and grandchildren. This one from the Topsham estate shows Joice, her son Robert and daughter Sarah, with Sarah's three daughters Ruthy, Joanna and Maria. According to her age of 28 years given on the 1817 register, Joice would have become a mother at 14 and a grandmother at 34, but it is possible her age was underestimated at first.

A three generation family tree at Topsham

Joice (born 1789)

Robert (b. 1803) — Sarah Bramwell (b. 1805)

Ruthy (b.1823) — Joanna Davy (b. 1827) — Maria (b. 1829)

Fathers

The observant reader will have noticed the lack of mention of fathers so far. This is because the status of 'slave' as property was passed on through the mother and therefore the identity of the fathers did not matter to the keepers of the Slave Registers, because they were recording assets on their estates. It also suggests that the mothers may not have been living in monogamous relationships in which the identity of the father could be assumed, therefore to name a father could be problematic. This leads on to the questions of what role men could play in the family under conditions of slavery, and then to what extent enslaved people lived in family groups, and whether these families were nuclear or matrifocal[45]. The Slave Registers for Topsham and Wear Pen are silent on this matter. While some 'slave marriages' are recorded for Manchester for the years 1821-1825[46], including some named Davy, matches for couples on these properties could not be found. The long term legacy of this erasure of the father from the records and the usurpation of his role as provider and authority figure has been enormous, with reverberations to this day in the phenomenon of the 'absent black father' in Caribbean communities on both sides of the Atlantic.

Racial categories[47]

Nevertheless, in recording the colour of enslaved people, the Topsham and Wear Pen registers were telling us something about the paternity and status of these individuals. The vast majority are recorded as 'negro', meaning full black, but occasionally there are 'mulattos' and 'sambos'. A mulatto in this social context is the child of a negro mother and white father (so half black, half white) and a sambo is the child of a negro parent and a mulatto parent (so three-quarters black and one quarter white). There were no 'quadroons' (one-quarter black, three quarters white) registered on these two estates.

---

45 Clarke, E. (1957). *My mother who fathered me: A study of the family in three selected communities in Jamaica.* London: Allen & Unwin. Patterson, O. (1969). *The sociology of slavery: An analysis of the origins, development, and structure of negro slave society in Jamaica.* New York: Humanities Press. Dunn, 2014.

46 Slave marriages/Manchester 1821-1825. CO137/162.

47 Here the language of the original documents is used, with the first mention of a racial term being in inverted commas. These terms are not acceptable today.

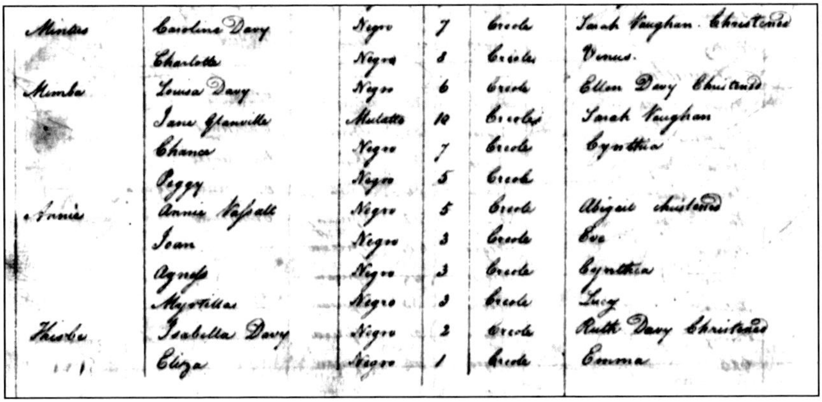

Minties	Caroline Davy	Negro	7	Creole	Sarah Vaughan Christened
	Charlotte	Negro	8	Creole	Venus.
Mimba	Louisa Davy	Negro	6	Creole	Ellen Davy Christened
	Jane Glanville	Mulatto	10	Creole	Sarah Vaughan
	Chance	Negro	7	Creole	Cynthia
	Peggy	Negro	5	Creole	
Annie	Annie Nassall	Negro	5	Creole	Abigail christened
	Joan	Negro	3	Creole	Eve
	Agnes	Negro	3	Creole	Cynthia
	Myrtilla	Negro	3	Creole	Lucy
Thisbe	Isabella Davy	Negro	2	Creole	Ruth Davy Christened
	Eliza	Negro	1	Creole	Emma

Extract from 1817 Wear Pen Slave Register showing mulatto, Jane Glanville (National Archives, Kew; obtained from Ancestry.com)

At Wear Pen, Mary Wilson had two sambo children: Ann Eliza Grigg (born 1824) and James Grigg (born 1826). Since Mary herself was negro, it appears that the father of these children was a mulatto with the surname Grigg, most likely an overseer employed on the estate. These sambo offspring would have had a slightly higher status than if they had been negroes but probably not high enough to absolve them of the heavy fieldwork of the other negroes. In the world of slavery, the lighter the colour the higher the status and the easier the life.

By contrast, the two mulatto children at Wear Pen would have been more fortunate. Jane Glanville (born 1807) and Lydia Davy (born 1828) were born to negro mothers (Sarah Vaughan and Chance Davy respectively) and white fathers. The father of Jane Glanville has been identified as Samuel Glanville, at that time probably an overseer at Wear Pen. As for Lydia Davy's father, he could have been one of the white Davy family. Perhaps access to more online records might enable us to find this out one day. These girls would have been likely to become house slaves, with a lighter workload and a closer relationship to their white owners.

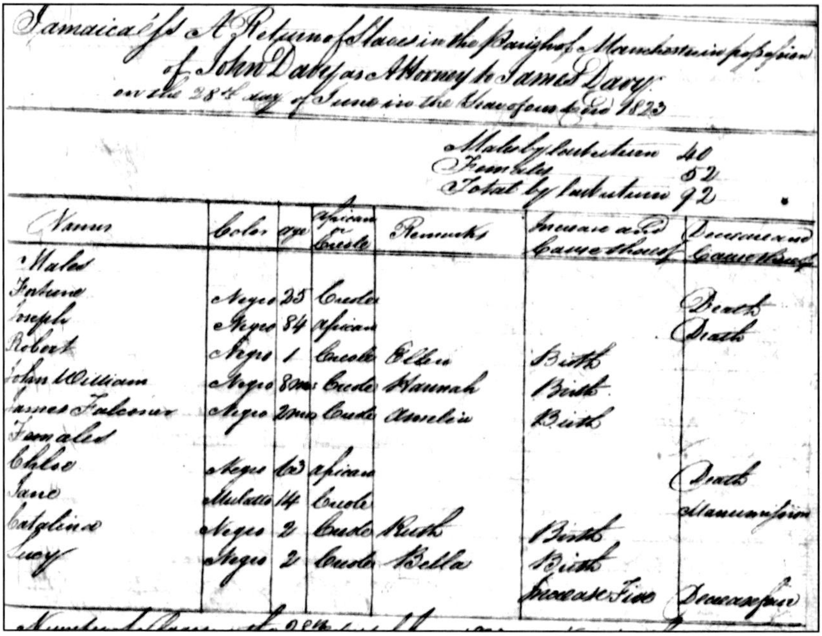

Jamaica ss. A Return of Slaves in the Parish of Manchester in possession of John Davy as Attorney to James Davy on the 28th day of June in the Year of our Lord 1823

Males by last return 40
Females do 52
Total by last return 92

Names	Color	Age	African or Creole	Remarks	Increase and Cause thereof	Decrease and Cause thereof
Males						
Fortune	Negro	35	Creole			Death
Joseph	Negro	84	African			Death
Robert	Negro	1	Creole	Ellen	Birth	
John William	Negro	8 mos	Creole	Hannah	Birth	
James Falconer	Negro	2 mos	Creole	Amelia	Birth	
Females						
Chloe	Negro	63	African			Death
Jane	Mulatto	14	Creole			Manumission
Catherine	Negro	2	Creole	Ruth	Birth	
Lucy	Negro	2	Creole	Bella	Birth	
					Increase Five	Decrease Five

Extract from 1823 Wear Pen Slave Register showing manumission of Jane (Glanville) (National Archives, Kew; obtained from Ancestry.com)

In this way the Jamaican colour/class system was born. Often depicted as a triangle, the small white elite at the top is separated from the mass of the black working class by the brown middle class. Descendants of the white slave-owners, the black enslaved, and the middle layer of the melange between the two still occupy similar status positions, albeit with much modification by the social and political changes in the nearly two centuries since Emancipation. The phenomenon of 'shadism' ('colourism'), or status based on lightness of complexion, is a related consequence of this early situation on estates such as the Davys'.

Manumission

Jane Glanville had the extra good fortune to obtain manumission, in other words, her freedom. This is shown in the 1823 Register for

Wear Pen, under 'decreases', where the manumission of fourteen-year-old Jane represents a loss on the books for the property, just as if she had died.

Manumission was not an easy process and was officially discouraged by the planter class as leading to both a loss of workers and the growth of a potentially dangerous class of 'free coloureds'. It required a legal process and usually the payment of the price of the enslaved person. I have not been able to find out exactly how and why Jane's manumission came about; although there are extensive transcriptions of manumission records on the website[48] for this era, the names Glanville and Davy are not there. Presumably it was Jane's father who wanted her freedom and paid her owner, James Davy, the price for her – this might have been any amount from 10s to £200 as seen from these records. But why at this time? It could have been because, in 1823, James Davy was winding up his affairs at Wear Pen and preparing to return to Devon, leaving his sons in charge. Perhaps he had been resisting manumitting Jane and his departure gave Samuel Glanville the chance to free her? Or had James promised Jane her freedom once he left, as though this was part of his will? There must have been an official record of this manumission and one day it may come to light. Jane Glanville was the only person manumitted from Topsham or Wear Pen over the years of the Slave Registers.

Resistance of enslaved people

History as it has been taught in Britain has not mentioned much about the resistance of the enslaved people, but they did not take their situation lightly. There were various ways of resisting oppression, from passive obstruction to active and organised rebellion, and the white owners only managed to keep their enslaved workers in a

---

48 Manumission of slaves in Jamaica p.1. National Archives CO137/162 from jamaicanfamilysearch.com.

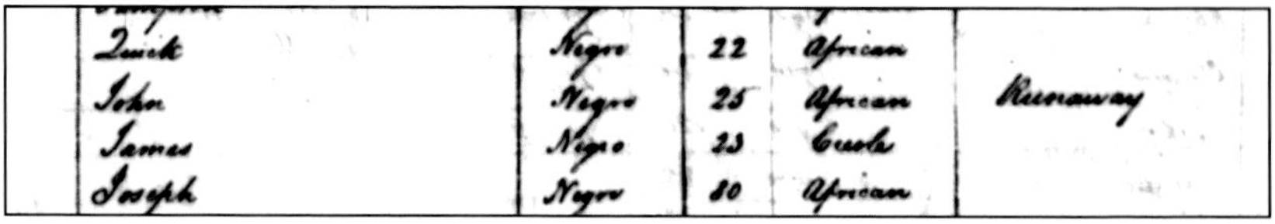

Quick	Negro	22	African	
John	Negro	25	African	Runaway
James	Negro	23	Creole	
Joseph	Negro	80	African	

Extract from 1817 Wear Pen Slave Register recording than John had run away (National Archives, Kew; obtained from Ancestry.com)

state of obedience by a regime of cruelty and close surveillance. The registers do not tell us what punishments were endured by enslaved people on Topsham and Wear Pen, but they do tell us about one young man who refused to accept his condition. This was John, an African aged 25 in 1817 at Wear Pen, who was listed as a runaway. Perhaps he tried to escape to the higher hills to join the Maroons, groups of people descended from former escapees who were able to live independently and avoid capture. However, his success did not last long as the 1820 Register now lists him as 'transported'. He must have been captured and probably brutally flogged before being transported off the island, perhaps to Cuba. One wonders whether this would have been a worse situation than the one he was already in?

In general, young African men were more likely to rebel than Creoles born in Jamaica. They were used to being free and less amenable to the restrictions imposed upon them. They spoke languages their captors did not understand and could communicate across distances through drumming, making their captors fear that they were plotting rebellion with those on other estates. For this reason, the whites, who lived in fear of a slave uprising, tried to mix Africans from different tribes who spoke different languages and who therefore could not communicate with each other, and put restrictions on drumming except for clearly recreational activities such as dancing. The relatively high proportion of Africans on the Davy estates would have exacerbated the whites' fears. As described earlier, the Slave Codes were designed to enable the whites to control their enslaved blacks, with stricter measures being introduced as enslaved people found ways to resist and rebel against their captivity. The role of the Davy men in controlling the black population will be described later.

In conclusion to Part 3, the Slave Registers tell us a great deal about the enslaved populations at Topsham and Wear Pen, their place of origin, births and deaths, names and races, freedom and rebellion. It is now time to turn back to focus on the Davy men, their roles in the system and their subsequent lives.

PART 4 ACTIVITIES OF JAMES AND JOHN DAVY IN JAMAICA

Military and civilian roles[49]

Military roles

The white planter class were seen as lazy and incompetent in most ways but in one way they were determined to succeed, and that was in uniting to control the black population, driven by fear of rebellion. That said, some measures that were supposed to be instituted were not. One of these was the ratio of whites to blacks on the plantations, which by a 1763 law was stipulated to be one white to every 30 blacks[50], but this was not often realised and fines were paid instead. Planters employed white overseers and book-keepers, such as Samuel Glanville at Wear Pen and Christopher Ramson at Topsham, to maintain the ratio. But the pressure was always on to have more enslaved field hands and it was not always possible to acquire enough white staff. Unfortunately we don't have records of these white overseers but a strong indication of the shortage can be found in the Royal Gazette for St Elizabeth of July 23rd, 1811, which reported that the estate of Edward Davy was fined *'because arms not sworn to*[51]. Presumably this refers to the Edward Davy of the Topsham estate who had died in about 1804 and no-one had taken his place in the militia.

The militia was the military organisation of white civilians organised on a local basis who were required by law to serve. The aim of the militia was to be ready to suppress slave uprisings. The Jamaica Almanacs record James Davy as being a captain in the

49 Information taken from the Jamaican Almanacs on jamaicanfamilysearch website

50 Deficiency Laws. Add. Ms. 12,404, fol.308.

51 Royal Gazette August 1811 (A Jamaican newspaper at the time)

Mandeville Court House, 2011 (Free Stock photo)

St Elizabeth regiment in 1808, followed by his son John in the Manchester regiment in 1824 as ensign, joined by John's brother, James Lewis Davy, in 1829 as captains; and by 1851 John was a major. The Davy men thus played their part in maintaining the privileged position of the planter class against the protests of the enslaved population. They would have been on high alert over the Christmas of 1831-2 at the time of the Sam Sharpe Rebellion (also called the Christmas Rebellion or the Baptist War), which was sparked on sugar plantations near Montego Bay and then spread rapidly across the island. This well organised rebellion helped put the nail in the coffin of the slavery system and hurried the passage of the 1833 Abolition Act back in Britain.

Civilian roles

The Davy men also played their part in the civilian government of Manchester. James Davy was a justice of the peace in St Elizabeth in 1801[52] and a magistrate in Manchester in 1817. By 1839, his son Dr James Lewis Davy had surpassed him and become the Custos Rotulorum for Manchester – i.e. the chief magistrate - while John served as an assistant magistrate[53]. In these roles they would have dispensed justice in line with the Slave Codes until Emancipation and after that by laws that did not distinguish by race on paper but which continued to serve the interests of the white planter class of the island. The court houses – especially the Mandeville court house built in 1817 to serve the parish of Manchester – were magnificent buildings at a time when the majority of the population lived in flimsy wattle and daub huts.

They also played a part in the Anglican Church, as shown by a document[54] recording the sale of six acres of land from Robert Crawford to Joseph Russell and James Davy, churchwardens, at May Day Pond next to Caledonia plantation. It appears that they were buying the land on behalf of the church for the newly formed parish of Manchester. They also donated a parcel of land next to Wear Pen for the building of St George's church.

In 1839, John and James Lewis Davy were both trustees of the newly formed Manchester Bank for Savings, an institution designed to encourage the newly emancipated Jamaicans to manage their money prudently, something of which they would have had very little previous experience.

The Davy men, father and sons, therefore played important roles in establishing and maintaining the economy and society of the parish of Manchester in the first half of the nineteenth century.

---

52 Families from Anglican Parish Registers and Wills, Descendants of George Ruggles, accessed on jamaicanfamilysearch.com.

53 Jamaicanfamilysearch.com/almanacs/Manchester

54 IRO Deed Liber 677, Folio 85, 1818.

John Davy's property interests

Of James Davy's three sons, John was the one who made his career in Jamaican property. As well as managing Wear Pen and Heavitree, he appears in various records in connection with many other properties in the area, as shown in this table.

Properties associated with John Davy

Property	Acres	1823	1826	1828	1831	1833	1838	1840	1845 J. Davis? receiver	Compensation received by
Allsides	2418					✓		✓		Admins
Asia	400					✓ rec				JD as rec
Berry Hill	624					✓				Ceal, Edwards, Palach
Blue Mountain	1700		✓ att	✓ att			✓			Mackeson
Bombay	?			✓ ?						
Devon	1500								✓	Denton as mortgagee
Grant's Green and Abingdon	400								✓	Peart
Green Hill	1065				✓ att	✓ att		✓	✓	
Green Pond	1657				✓ att	✓ att				
Green Vale 2	600				✓ att	✓ att	✓	✓	✓	
Hanbury and Russell Place	2935		att	✓ att	✓ att	✓ att	✓ att	✓		Parke

Property	Acres	1823	1826	1828	1831	1833	1838	1840	1845 J. Davis? receiver	Compensation received by
King's Land and Hopeton	980								✓	Many
Knowsley Park	656				✓	✓ att		✓	✓	T. Davy
Litchfield	631			✓ adm	✓ adm	✓ adm		✓		Wilson
Lyndhurst	1275							✓		Ricketts
Parke Hall	Not on LBS					✓ ?				
Robin's Hall	688	✓ own	✓ own	✓ own	✓ own					Trustees for Campbell
Ross Hill	396 Not on LBS								✓	
Skiddaw	300							✓?		
Vauxhall	Not on LBS			✓						
Weare Pen and Heavitree	1724			✓ own	✓ own	✓ own	✓ own	✓ own	✓ own	John Davy and James L Davy
Total		1	3	7	8	11	4	9	8	

Key[55]: adm = administrator; att = attorney; own = beneficial owner; rec = receiver; LBS = Legacies of British Slavery website (ucl.ac.uk/lbs); ? = unclear association

55 For an explanation of these terms see www.ucl.ac.uk/lbs/project/individuals.

This table puts together information from the Jamaican Almanacs, the Legacies of British Slavery website and the Slave Registers on the properties in Manchester with which John Davy had some association. The Almanacs list properties and their owners on a two-yearly basis by parish. The 'owner' is not precisely defined so can be a receiver, administrator, executor or even attorney, as well as the beneficial owner. The ticks (✓) in the table show where John Davy is listed as 'owner' in the Almanacs. This information is supplemented by data given on the LBS website under 'Estates', which were derived from the Slave Registers and Crop Accounts (accounts sent by attorneys to absentee owners, now found in the Jamaican National Archives in Spanish Town). The information from these sources is incomplete and sometimes contradictory but, as far as possible, they denote where he was the attorney, the receiver, the administrator or the beneficial owner. He is counted as the beneficial owner where he signed as owner on the Slave Register or received the compensation money at Emancipation.

Using these criteria, he was only the beneficial owner of his half share of Wear Pen and Heavitree with his brother James Lewis Davy, for which they received compensation in 1835 from the British government; he received compensation as receiver for Asia; and although he signed the Slave Register as owner for Robin's Hall the compensation reverted to the child of the previous owner, throwing into doubt whether John was owner at all.

What the table shows is that John Davy started to extend his interest in other properties from 1823 when his father James was still in Jamaica and owner of Wear Pen. At this point John 'purchased' Robin's Hall with its 42 enslaved workers. In the next two years he became attorney to Blue Mountain and Hanbury and Russell Place. By 1828 his father had died and John had inherited a half share in Wear Pen and Heavitree with this elder brother James Lewis; he also had some unspecified association with Bombay, Litchfield and Vauxhall. As the end of slavery approached in 1831 and estate owners faced a financial crisis, it seems that John expanded his operations and became attorney to several more estates – Green Hill, Green Pond and Green Vale – and possibly his Uncle Thomas' Knowsley Park. In 1833, the last year of slavery records, John had his largest list of properties, eleven altogether, when he added Allsides, Berry Hill and Parke Hall in an unclear capacity, became receiver for Asia, and definitely became attorney for Knowsley Park and Litchfield.

By 1838, the period of post-slavery apprenticeship was ending (see later); record-keeping was probably chaotic and John is only recorded under four properties. The LBS records cease after compensation was paid (1835) so there is less information available from this time. In 1840 the Almanacs give him as 'owner' of nine properties in an unclear capacity but they make it clear in 1845 that he was the receiver for the remaining eight properties.

These records show that John Davy was active during the time around Emancipation when slave-owners were in financial difficulties and many facing bankruptcy. It is not clear whether he was receiver in a private or official capacity. Was he speculating in property and did he make much money from it? Why did he become attorney for so many estates – and how could he physically manage this task when presumably he would have to travel over rugged terrain on horseback before the days of roads and railways to manage these plantations tens of miles apart?

Hoping to gain more insight into his activities and motivation, I sought the help of friends, Richard and Marjorie-Anne Howe (a lawyer and a historian), to transcribe and interpret some old indentures of which Geoffrey Davy had obtained copies from the Island Record Office in Spanish Town. Six of these relate to John Davy's land deals, as shown in this table.

John Davy's land deals

Date	Folio	Description
1826	186[56]	John Davy seems to be conveying his half share in Wear Pen, inherited on the 1825 death of his father, James, to John Coley. Refers to James Davy's 1821 will. Could it have been as a surety to raise money to buy Robin's Hall? Coley was attorney at the Topsham estate 1823.
1833	87[57]	'Release'. Jane Levens of Litchfield releases John Davy from her legal case against him for not paying her annuity after the death of her husband. Davy was joint administrator with Jane Levens and agent for Wm Parke and Richard Hall to whom the estate was indebted.
1852	143[58]	Mortgage from Thomas Anderson to John Davy of Spring Plain on Clarendon/Manchester border. It appears that Anderson is in debt to Davy and using his property as surety for this unpaid debt of £696.
1854	126[59]	Sale of land, part of Bushy Park to south of Wear Pen, from George Saunders to John Davy. This would have been to enlarge Wear Pen.
1857	218[60]	Conveyance of insolvent estate, The Cedars, in St Catherine (formerly called Mount Pleasant) to John Davy from Alfred Melhado and Philip Clarke for £1100.
1860	74[61]	Conveyance of Crawford's Pen in St Elizabeth from John Blair to John Davy in 1836. This transaction was only completed in 1860 when John Davy was returning to England.

56 LOS Deeds Liber 740 folio 186

57 LOS Deeds Liber 786 folio 87

58 LOS Deeds Liber 907 folio 143

59 LOS Deeds Liber 914 folio 126

60 LOS Deeds Liber 925 folio 218

61 LOS Deeds Liber 930 folio 74

These six transactions cover the period from the death of John's father James (1825) to the probable ill health of John and his return to England (1860). Only one of them corresponds with the information on John's property interests from the earlier table, the 1833 'Release'. This document relates to a property called Litchfield owned by the Levens. It states that Jane's husband George Levens had died intestate and without issue in 1823, leaving Litchfield indebted to merchants William Parke and Richard Hall. Davy was an agent for Parke and Hall and, on George's death, John Davy became joint administrator of his estate with Jane Levens. However, several matters of dispute arose between them which resulted in his not paying her the annuity to which, as widow, she was entitled by law. This led to her beginning legal processes to sue Parke and Hall, and Davy, in the Court of Chancery. This document seems to be an out of court settlement by which Parke and Hall, and Davy, agree to pay the amount of annuity owed, plus interest, and Jane Levens agrees to drop the cases and not to interfere with Davy's management of Litchfield. This document, therefore, gives some interesting insight into the complications of John Davy's property dealings.

The information in the two tables above indicates John Davy's extensive activities in the business of land acquisition and management during and after the slavery period in central Jamaica. In the 1820s and 30s, when he was a young man, he appears to have done a deal using his own inherited share of Wear Pen to possibly buy his own property of Robin's Hall. He became attorney on several properties fairly local to Wear Pen, sometimes as agent to merchants to whom the owners owed money. As estates' financial difficulties mounted at the time of Emancipation, he became administrator or receiver for more properties. Two decades later, now in his fifties with possibly declining health and planning to return to England, he seemed to be in a strong financial position and was buying up indebted properties and calling in debts owed to him by others.

What was John Davy like? Did plantation owners fear seeing him arrive up their driveways on his horse? He must have been a strong and forceful character if he was able to successfully manage so many different enterprises at a time of great change and conflict in the slavery system. He was probably very driven, given the more academic example of his older brother, James Lewis, and the outstanding business success of his younger brother, George (see later). Many of the Davy men had this entrepreneurial streak that enabled them to adapt to whatever opportunity was available at the time and muscle their way towards the top of the heap!

The next section of the story goes back a few years to look more closely at Emancipation of the enslaved workers and its consequences for the newly freed, the local economy and the Davy family.

PART 5 AFTER SLAVERY

Emancipation and its aftermath

As explained earlier, it had been expected by campaigners against the slave trade, such as William Wilberforce, that the end of the supply of new Africans would force West Indian planters to improve conditions of enslavement. The programme of Amelioration went some way towards achieving this aim, but not far enough. This led to a revival of the anti-slavery campaign in Britain and a demand for the end of the institution of slavery itself. Increasing unrest, such as the Sam Sharpe Rebellion, mentioned earlier, put further pressure on the British Parliament to legislate to end the 'peculiar institution'. It has also been argued [62] that it had become possible to end slavery at this time because it had become less profitable and also less valuable to the British economy as colonial expansion in India and industrialisation at home had taken over from sugar as pillars of the economy. The Slavery Abolition Act was passed in the British Parliament in 1833 after a lengthy battle against the powerful pro-slavery West Indian lobby. This ended slavery in the British West Indies from 1 August 1834 though full freedom had to wait until 1838 after a period of Apprenticeship, a time supposedly to prepare the formerly enslaved population for their freedom but actually an extension of semi-slavery for a further four years. Originally planned to last six years, protests and unrest of the 'apprentices' brought forward the end of this phase by two years. The first of August is now celebrated as Emancipation Day across the English-speaking Caribbean.

Compensation

It was only by compensating the slave-owners for their human

---

62 Williams, E. (1944). *Capitalism and slavery.* University of North Carolina Press.

property that it was possible to pass the Act due to the powerful West India lobby in the British parliament. Approximately £20 million compensation was paid to slave-owners for their roughly 800,000 enslaved people. This amounted to an average of about £25 per head, worth perhaps eighty times as much in today's money (£2,000). The exact worth of each person depended on factors such as their age, sex, physical fitness, and the profitability of the particular colony. These payments came from the British taxpayer, who continued to pay until 2015 when the debt was at last paid off. Nothing was paid to the formerly enslaved people for their years of toil and suffering, or given to them to help them start a new life of freedom.

The compensation records are kept in the National Archives at Kew and have been made public on the Legacies of British Slavery (LBS) website hosted by University College, London. From these we can learn how much money the Davy men received for their enslaved people. Regarding the Topsham estate, the compensation records do not distinguish it from Knowsley Park (seven miles to the north) as their estate accounts were combined; Rebecca had died and left her share of Topsham and Knowsley Park to her brother, Dr Thomas Davy of Ottery St Mary, who received £1,100 for his 59 enslaved people. John and James Lewis Davy received £2,156 between them for the 106 enslaved people at Wear Pen and Heavitree. This was typical for owners of medium-sized coffee plantations and pens, or shared sugar plantations.

How did the Davy compensation payments compare with those of other Devon slave-owners?

These payments of just over £1,000 each put the Davy men in the middle group of Devon slave-owners[63]. Out of the 78 recipients of

63 Allen, G.M. (2021). A typology of Devon slave-owners. In *Transactions of the Devonshire Association, 154.*

compensation money residing in Devon in 1835, 41 received less and 36 received more than Thomas Davy. Those receiving less than £1,000 included those (mainly women) who had a small number of enslaved domestic workers or a small coffee plantation, but a number were men who had inherited a large sugar plantation and become indebted so that the compensation went to their creditors. Those who received more were owners of sugar plantations or merchants to whom planters were mortgaged. Examples of those receiving less are Margaret Taylor of Dawlish, herself a woman of colour, who owned one enslaved person in Jamaica and who received £29; Elizabeth Rowe of Kentisbury who had a share of a coffee plantation and received £602; and then William Vassall of Berry Pomeroy who received nothing for the 198 enslaved people on his Jamaican sugar plantation because he was indebted to his London merchant. Examples of those receiving more include Alexander Hamilton Hamilton of The Retreat, Topsham, Devon, who received £3,784 for 140 enslaved people on his two sugar estates in Grenada, and Henry Porter of Winslade House, Clyst St Mary, who was awarded £35,961 for 709 enslaved people on his large sugar plantation in Guyana. This range of amounts of compensation money indicate the position of the Davy men in the status hierarchy of West Indian slave-owners; not vastly wealthy nabobs but very comfortably off.

Change in agriculture after Emancipation

After Emancipation the former system of slave-based export agriculture became much less profitable; there was widespread abandonment of sugar and coffee plantations and a rapid growth of peasant agriculture[64]. Between 1832 and 1847 over half of Jamaican coffee plantations were abandoned, including 109 in Manchester. Livestock pens and pimento walks, however, continued, along

[64] Higman (1988).

with peasant smallholdings growing foodstuffs on marginal land. Higman shows a 1858 plan of how a former coffee plantation adjacent to Knowsley Park, called Devon (owned by Margaretta Davy – see later), was divided into small lots which were rented out, perhaps to formerly enslaved people. These had grassland for cattle, pimento walks and some coffee, as well as food gardens. One large section is called 'Davy piece' and consists of 'pimento and rent land'. It would be interesting to know whether the other Davy properties had been divided up like this too.

What became of the formerly enslaved people?

Once their workers had to be paid a wage, the planters tried their best to keep them tied to the plantations and working long hours in near slavery conditions, for example by charging extortionate rents on houses and by restricting the right to market home-grown crops. In response, those who could, moved off the plantations and up to higher ground in the hills to attempt to live independently by subsistence agriculture[65], though with no access to land rights, capital or training this was not easy. Nevertheless there was a general movement of population from the lowland sugar plantations to the hills. This led to a spectacular growth in freehold smallholdings of under 50 acres from 2,800 in 1840 to 130,000 by 1900[66]. Only the most destitute ex-slaves stayed as labourers on the plantations.

During this time (1844 – 1900) the black population of the island doubled[67]. Census figures give the Jamaican population as 380,000 in 1844 and 730,000 in 1900, of which the largest proportion were black. This presents a contrast to the steady decline under conditions of slavery and gives the lie to the planters' contentions

65 Sherlock, P. and Bennett, H. (1998). *The story of the Jamaican people.* Kingston, Jamaica: Ian Randle.

66 Higman (1988)

67 Higman (1988)

about black women not having a maternal instinct.

The resettlement of the formerly enslaved population was assisted by the establishment of 'free villages' with help from some non-conformist groups who raised money in Britain for the purchase of land which was divided into small lots. One of the first free villages was Maidstone, founded in 1838 near to the Topsham property by Moravian missionaries[68]. When I visited in 2007 I met Sergeant Enue 'Sas'

Sergeant Sass Davey at his grandfather's house 2007 (Photo by friend of author)

The author and Davey family members at the family burial plot 2007 (Photo by friend of author)

---

[68] Sutherland, A. Welcome to Maidstone: Historic Manchester community eyes heritage tourism. *Jamaica Observer*, Aug 13, 2012.

Davey, retired from the Jamaica Defence Force, who showed us the still thriving Moravian church in which he was heavily involved, the remains of the nearby Topsham property house where Edward Davy would have lived, the remains of the Sergeant's great-grandfather's house and two well-maintained cemeteries of Davey graves. These black Daveys were presumably descendants of enslaved Africans on the Davy plantation who had adopted the surname 'Davy' when they were christened in 1820 and later changed the spelling to add the 'e'. They had managed to survive and multiply, testifying to the worthwhile influence of the free villages. My former colleague, Mrs Davey, was the sister-in-law of Sas Davey – that is how the link between the Countess Wear and Jamaican Davys (Daveys) was made!

The inscriptions on these tombstones go right back to the first post-slavery generation with Sergeant Davey's great-grandfather, George Davey, born 1839. A freedom baby! The family in the photograph were having a work day to maintain their family plot to a high standard in keeping with the prestigious pink granite gravestones that their relatives, now living in the USA, had sent over.

There are only three individuals who were formerly 'property' of the Davys whom I have managed to trace from slavery into their later lives. Two of these were Jane Glanville and Caroline Davy, both daughters of Sarah Vaughan of Wear Pen and mentioned in the 1862 will of Samuel Glanville[69]. As mentioned earlier, Jane Glanville was Samuel Glanville's manumitted mulatto daughter. He now refers to her as Jane Peart, wife of Joseph Peart, and leaves her a £26 annuity; a small amount but no doubt a great help to her in her later years. To Caroline Davy, the 'negro' sister of Jane, Samuel refers to her having lived for many years at his residence, Greenvale, and expresses the wish that she be allowed to continue

69 Exemplification of the will of Samuel Glanville. IRO wills Manchester Vol 129, p.124-126.

grazing her livestock there. It appears that he had given her some help after Emancipation in accommodating her and perhaps giving her some livestock enabling her to build up capital to live an independent life. Near the end of her life she is listed in the 1878 Manchester Parish Directory as *'keeper of a lodging house'*. Neither of these women was forced to continue a life of labour on a plantation but were able to rise to a more middle class position.

The third one is based on contradictory information. The BBC's 'Who do you think you are?' programme, which aired on 10/09/2008, traced the ancestors of TV chef Ainsley Harriot back to Wear Pen. It claimed that his ancestry could be traced back to Catherine Smith, born in 1830, daughter of enslaved Joan Davy and white overseer Jonathan Briggs (Griggs?), but this does not tie in with the slave registers because Catherine Smith is recorded as being 'negro' not 'mulatto' as she would have been if her parentage was as claimed. Perhaps the BBC researchers had access to other information? Or there are mistakes or deliberate falsifications on the slave registers?

How reliable are the slave registers anyway? If Briggs wanted to conceal his paternity of the child, he could give her a surname that was not his – as it seems he did by calling her 'Smith' not 'Briggs'. Furthermore, the registers were sworn to by the owner – in this case John Davy – in front of the visiting magistrate who was

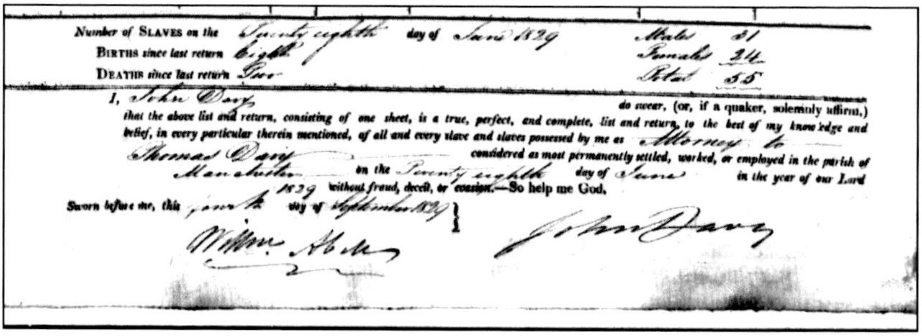
Number of SLAVES on the Twenty eighth day of June 1829 Males 31
BIRTHS since last return Eight Females 24
DEATHS since last return Two Total 55
I, John Davy, do swear, (or, if a quaker, solemnly affirm,) that the above list and return, consisting of one sheet, is a true, perfect, and complete, list and return, to the best of my knowledge and belief, in every particular therein mentioned, of all and every slave and slaves possessed by me as Attorney to Thomas Davy considered as most permanently settled, worked, or employed in the parish of Manchester on the Twenty eighth day of June in the year of our Lord 1829 without fraud, deceit, or evasion.—So help me God.
Sworn before me, this day of September 1829
John Davy

Topsham Slave Register 1829 showing signatures (National Archives, Kew; obtained from Ancestry.com)

generally a neighbouring slave-owner. This excerpt from Wear Pen's 1829 register shows that the Davys' friend from Alphington (near Exeter, England) and owner of Devon Pen, William Abell, was the magistrate. Easy, therefore, to cheat the system. Nevertheless, Higman[70] claims that on the whole the figures in the registers show little evidence of concealment and they succeeded in their primary purpose, that of suppressing the illegal importation of Africans.

The paths of the former enslavers also took new turns following the end of slavery.

Dr Thomas Davy of Ottery St Mary and his descendants

Family trees 2 and 3 in the Appendix show some of the descendants of the white Davy family.

Thomas Davy (1773/4 – 1852) has been mentioned already as inheriting the Topsham plantation on the death of his elder brother, Edward, in 1804. Thomas was an absentee owner and there is no evidence that he ever visited his Jamaican property, instead leaving it to be managed by his brother James and later by John Coley. The Almanacs are not clear as to whether the person 'in possession' is the owner or the attorney, and the estate accounts combine Topsham with Knowsley Park, so it is difficult to disentangle them.

Thomas was born in Countess Wear and moved to Ottery St Mary to practice medicine. He lived at various houses in Ottery, eventually settling in the Raleigh House, probably the town's most prestigious house, on Mill Street. He married Elizabeth Boutflower by whom he had many children, several dying in infancy. Thomas, Elizabeth and several of their children are buried in the Ottery St Mary churchyard where they are commemorated by a large flat tomb towards the south-west corner. An oil painting of him, in the possession of Australian great great granddaughter, Lesley

70 Higman (1976).

Raleigh House, Ottery St Mary, Devon, UK (Photo by author)

Morton, was reproduced in the Express and Echo (Exeter's local newspaper) on April 16, 2002. Thomas clearly spent some of his profits from slavery in acquiring this house - and also in educating his sons.

Dr Thomas Davy of Raleigh House (Source: Lesley Morton, Australia)

The blue plaque on the Raleigh House commemorates one of Thomas' sons, Edward (1806 – 1885), a scientist and inventor. It does not tell us the source of the income which allowed him the education and leisure to become a scientist. As told by a descendant in Australia[71], Edward followed his interests in chemistry and physics, and invented a device for relaying electrical signals over long distances – essential for the development of the railways in the 1830s. As luck would have it, he had a bad marriage with a legal case from which he had to escape, rushing off to Australia in 1839 and leaving his father to patent his invention. But Thomas does not seem to have inherited the entrepreneurial spirit of the other Davys, and he left the apparatus to rot in a field[72]. In the meantime, another scientist (Wheatstone) had patented a similar invention and it was his that was taken up by the railways. Edward nevertheless carved out a varied and interesting life for himself in Australia, establishing a starch factory, a distillery, editing a regional newspaper, and becoming assay master for testing the purity of gold in the gold rush, making a significant contribution to the development of the colony[73].

One of Thomas' daughters, Mary Ann Davy (1800-1857), seems to have been an adventurous woman because she took herself off to Jamaica, where an M. Davy is recorded as owning (or managing?) Bellefield and Cumberland properties in 1845. She died at Knowsley Park in 1857 and is buried at St George's Church at Wear Pen[74]. There must be some family link to the William Davy who owned Bellefield and had died there in 1851 but I have not been able to identify his relationship to the rest of the family. This

71 Davey, J. (2005). Edward Davy – his life in South Australia. In *Heritage: Journal of the Ottery St Mary Heritage Society*, Winter 2005.

72 Homer, R. (2005). Edward Davy (1806-1885) Ottery's pioneer of the electric telegraph. In *Heritage: Journal of the Ottery St Mary Heritage Society*, Spring 2005.

73 Davey, J. (2005).

74 Monumental Inscriptions of Jamaica, accessed on jamaicanfamilysearch.com

is a mystery waiting to be investigated.

Thomas also had an eminent grandson in Sir Henry Davy (1855-1922), physician at the Royal Devon and Exeter Hospital (RD&E), president of the local BMA in 1907 and sheriff of Exeter in 1887. His obituary states: *'He was a cheerful, hearty man, given to hospitality and acts of kindness, a keen fly-fisherman, and a collector of old English china*[75].

Thomas Davy benefitted from his ownership of enslaved Africans on his Topsham and Knowsley Park estates in Jamaica. He was able to live in the most prominent house in Ottery and to educate his sons to occupy professional positions which raised their status and contributed to the wider British and Australian societies. He may not have broadcast the source of his wealth; possibly he had mixed feelings about it. He did not sign the 1814 Ottery petition against the resumption of the French slave trade when most other prominent citizens did so, suggesting that he recognised his complicity in the iniquitous system.

Descendants of James Davy of Wear Pen

Dr James Lewis Davy (1799-1840)

James' eldest son, James Lewis Davy M.D., only appears as an adult in the Jamaican records in 1839, when he is Custos Rotolorum (chief magistrate) of Manchester and captain in the Manchester Militia. Although he shared ownership of Wear Pen with his brother John there is no evidence that he played an active part in managing the plantation. And yet he is referred to as *'of the Island of Jamaica'* when he got married in Torquay (then called Tormoham) in 1834[76]. Through this marriage to the widowed Margaretta

---

75 Lancet, 1922.

76 England, Devon Bishop's Transcripts 1558-1887, DRO. Accessed on FamilySearch.

Parsons Abell he acquired her 1800 acre property of Devon Pen (Jamaica), previously referred to. Sadly, James did not live long and died childless in Kingston in 1840.

There is a story here: in fact, several. Margaretta (1794 - 1873) was the daughter of Rev William Neyle of Ambrook House, Ipplepen, himself a slave-owner, and in 1820 she married William Abell, son of Francis Abell of Alphington and owner of Devon Pen in Manchester, Jamaica[77]. She went with him and left behind her beautiful childhood home in a charming Devon valley to move to an even more magnificent area, in Jamaica, on a knoll surrounded by a ring of green hills and fertile plantations. She had several children with William but he died on board ship returning to England in 1833[78]. Perhaps she was also on the ship as, a few months later, she was in Torquay marrying James Lewis Davy. Margaretta (now) Davy died at 44, Magdalen Street, Exeter, in 1873; she was probably being treated at the nearby Royal Devon and Exeter hospital[79]

Ambrook House, Christiana, Jamaica, 2011 (Photo by author)

Ambrook is an unusual name, so when I took a friend to visit Ambrook House in Ipplepen, she was amazed as she had lived in an Ambrook House in

---

77 England, Devon and Cornwall Marriages 1660-1912. Accessed on FamilySearch.

78 Western Times, Feb 9, 1833.

79 Daily Gleaner excerpts 1873 from jamaicanfamilysearch.com. Thanks to Angela Dodd-Crompton for these references.

Christiana, Jamaica. Could there be a connection? Of course there must be, though I have yet to establish it firmly. Christiana is the town closest to the Devon Pen where Margaretta lived – so did she build a townhouse and name it after her childhood home? It seems very likely!

The story of Margaretta is exciting to me as linking three Devon families in their ventures in Jamaica. William Abell and Samuel Glanville were partners before the latter obtained his own Greenvale property. Glanville was originally employed by James Davy on Wear Pen and his family was later helped by Dr Thomas Davy of Ottery St Mary on their 1851 return to England. And now James Lewis Davy married Abell's widow, Margaretta. Her story illustrates the social networks that criss-crossed the Atlantic and supported families in this era of uncertainty and high mortality. Such networks were a strong element of slave-owning families across Britain and include, to give Devon examples, the Rowe/James/Williams/Hovenden family[80], and the D'Urban/Mitchell/Porter and Trefusis/Adams/Rolle families[81].

John Davy (1801-1863) and his descendants

John Davy married Emma Maria de Verte (1820 - 1902) in London in 1841 but their five children were all born in Jamaica: Mary Eliza (b. 1844), John (b.1846), James Stewart (1848-1915), Emma Fanny (1852-1902), and Charlotte Anne (b.1856), twin to Thomas George (1856-1909). In about 1860 John wound up his affairs in Jamaica and returned with his young family to England, but now he was wealthy enough to move to a fashionable area of London, not to the relative obscurity of Countess Wear. The 1861 census shows the family living at 25, Royal Crescent, Kensington, a newly built crescent of grand houses near to Hyde Park. However,

80 Personal communication from Di Cooper

81 Personal communication from Peter Wingfield-Digby

John's health must have been compromised and he died two years later, in 1863, at the age of 62, leaving Emma Maria with the five children ranging in age from seven to nineteen years old. This must have been a difficult time for her, emotionally and financially, as the next census, of 1871, shows her living in a much more modest home, at 69 Shirland Road, Paddington[82]. She died in Haywards Heath, Sussex, near the home of her son James.

John Davy's house at Royal Crescent, Kensington, London (Photo by author)

An enchanting photograph held by descendants of John Davy is this one of his youngest son, Thomas George, in the arms of his nurse, possibly taken soon after the family arrived in London. Her name (from the 1861 census) is Rachel Longmore, born in Jamaica in 1828. Rachel is another link between Davy and Glanville families, as she had a daughter by James Glanville at Greenvale (Manchester, Jamaica) yet here she was, working as a nurse to the Davy family in London! She

Thomas G. Davy held by Rachel Longmore (Source: Geoffrey Davy, Australia)

---

82 Davy, G.J.G. (2013).

must have left her daughter, Mary Ann Caroline Glanville[83], born 1851, in Jamaica when she left for London, an early example of a pattern that would be followed in the Windrush generation of the twentieth century. Rachel does not appear in later UK censuses so we hope she was able to return to her daughter when her tour of duty was over.

Was Rachel born enslaved? Her date of birth, before Emancipation, makes it a possibility but I have not found her name on any slave register, or on any other baptism register, so the question remains open.

Sir James Stewart Davy (1848-1915)

Another of John Davy's sons was James Stewart who, along with his younger brother, Thomas George, was educated at Uppingham public school followed by Oxford University. James' obituary in Who's Who 1915 records the highlights of his career:

"He was called to the Bar in England and entered on the Poor Law Service. In 1876 he became Assistant General Inspector and two years later General Inspector for Yorkshire, and in 1905 Chief Inspector. He was made a C.B. (Companion of the Bath) in 1902 and a K.C.B. (Knight Commander of the Bath) nine years later."

As he entered the Poor Law service at almost the same time as it was re-organised in 1871 with the abolition of the Poor Law Board and the absorption of its functions into the Local Government Board, he was able to play a major role in its administration, as detailed in a 1913 Spectator article: '*Certainly no Poor Law official has left a greater and more permanent mark on Poor Law administration than*

83 Jamaica Church of England Parish Register Transcripts 1664-1880. Accessed on FamilySearch.

he.'[84]. With our very negative modern views on the workhouse as a key part of the nineteenth century Poor Law, one wonders whether Sir James managed to improve these institutions during his tenure.

But perhaps James is not as well remembered today as his wife, Lady Joanna Charlotte Davy, who became a serious botanist after the family moved to Cuckfield, Sussex, in 1893. Here she led plant-hunting expeditions and contributed to knowledge of local flora. Some of her plant specimens are held at Kew Gardens and some of her watercolours of orchids are in the Natural History Museum[85].

This Davy couple, then, contributed to British social development in the late nineteenth century and to the science of botany. James' education was funded by his father's profits from the system of slavery in Jamaica, but he no doubt put in his own hard work and talent, as did his wife.

Thomas George Davy (1856-1909)

John Davy's youngest son was Thomas George, born in Jamaica but moved to England with his family as a young child; he is shown in the arms of his nurse, Rachel Longmore, in the photograph above, probably taken in Royal Crescent, Kensington. He was educated at Uppingham School, followed by Exeter College, Oxford, from which he graduated as a Bachelor of Arts in 1880[86], and then began to study medicine, eventually becoming an M.D. (Oxon) in 1894. He is said, in family lore, to have travelled as a doctor to several Far Eastern countries before settling down with his wife, nurse Emily née Gates, whom he married in Hokitika, New Zealand,

---

84 archive.spectator.co.uk/article/22nd-november-1913/14/sir-james-davy-kcb

85 https://en.wikipedia.org/wiki/Joanna_Charlotte_Davy

86 Alumni Oxonienses:The Members of the University of Oxford 1715-1886, by Joseph Foster

in 1885[87]. He had probably joined the Colonial Medical Service and been sent to these far-flung outposts of the British Empire to minister to colonial officials. After leaving the CMS Thomas had a medical practice in Kumara, South Island, New Zealand (1886-1890), which was the site of the last gold rush and already a town in decline.

From New Zealand, documents held by his descendants illuminate his subsequent life. He moved to the new gold rush town of Coolgardie in Western Australia where he specialised in the infectious diseases that ran rife among prospectors in this desert area. It must have been a rough life but Thomas seems to have been a tough character. Emily may have helped him as a nurse, or perhaps caring for their four children born over the years 1887-1896 may have absorbed all her energy.

The family was later able to move to more comfortable climes in Freemantle (1901) then Perth (1903), where Thomas became a resident doctor at the Perth Hospital and held several extra public health positions in an attempt to earn a better income. Eventually, after much correspondence with the Health Department, his salary was raised from £250 to £450. He was one of the first names on the Western Australian Medical Register and became president of the British Medical Association (W.A. Branch). His obituary in The Medical Directory for 1909 extols his intellect, athleticism and independence of character. *"A medico with the highest qualifications, one of the best-read men in the State and a walking encyclopaedia on literary subjects…rather out of place among the crude conditions of the colonial community."* His public school and Oxford education made him stand out and no doubt helped him to gain high status in this young colony. It was Thomas who made the transition from being born in Jamaica as the son of a slave-owner to pioneer doctor in

87 New Zealand Civil Records Indexes 1800-1966

the rough conditions of Western Australia. Subsequent generations have found this State to be to their liking and have built good lives there.

Geoffrey (born 1933), the Australian referred to at the beginning of this story, is Dr Thomas George's grandson. He is a cattle rancher in Albany, Western Australia. Geoffrey has researched his family extensively and written this up, together with his own story, in: 'The Davy Family: Gaius 1633 to Ebony Rae 2012' published by Xlibris. Geoffrey has several children, grandchildren and great-grandchildren living nearby. It is Geoffrey who took the initiative to visit Countess Wear and Jamaica in 2011.

To what extent did the Western Australian Davys benefit from the slave-ownership of their forebears? Dr Thomas George did not directly inherit anything from his mother Emma (widow of slave-owner, John Davy), as her 1902 will mentions her other four children but not Thomas[88]. Why was he excluded? Had there been a rift in the family, or was it because he was so far away from the UK at that time? Thomas had had money invested in his education at school, university and his medical training – did his mother think this was enough? But perhaps this education was more valuable to him and his children than a monetary inheritance would have been because it enabled him to establish the family among the social elite of Perth. In later years these social connections, especially through marriage, were vital in giving Thomas' sons and grandchildren, including Geoffrey and his sister Primrose, a leg-up when misfortunes struck the family.

Descendants of George Thomas Davy (1803-1874)

The youngest son of James Davy of Wear Pen, was George Thomas Davy, whose family has been researched by a descendant, Catriona

---

88 A copy of Emma Davy's will is in the possession of Geoffrey Davy

Davy[89]. George made a fortune in the early days of the guano boom in Chile and his son, George Baynton Davy (1838 – 1907), used his inheritance to buy and develop Spean Lodge in Scotland, near to Fort William. Here the family lived a life of leisure. Their photographs can be seen on the website ww.speanlodge.co.uk. Clearly George Thomas was a man of great business acumen who saw an early opportunity in guano and made a success of it. One wonders to what extent early financial input from Wear Pen had assisted the establishment of his business?

Mixed-race Davy descendants

Going back to John Davy of Wear Pen, he was married in 1841 at the age of 40; what happened before that? There are other Davys who claim descent from John Davy 'on the wrong side of the blanket'. It has not been possible to verify these claims from the written records but illegitimate births were not necessarily recorded in Jamaica in those days. This particular family who gave me information illustrates the effects of the post World War II Windrush exodus on a mixed-race Jamaican family.

One of these mixed-race descendants, from South London, is the daughter of Herbert Davy who travelled to England in 1960 as part of the Windrush generation. Herbert used to live in Christiana (already mentioned as in northern Manchester, Jamaica, and near to Devon Pen, location of Ambrook House) and already had children when he emigrated. These children were left behind in Jamaica and he started a new family when he arrived in England, of whom Valerie is one. Valerie informed me that she had family

---

89 Personal communication, Geoffrey Davy

Davys meet at Christiana, Jamaica, 2011 (Photo by author)

House of mixed-race Davy family (Photo by author)

members who still farmed at Devon Pen and, on my visit to the area in 2011 with Geoffrey and Primrose Davy from Australia, we went to look for these relatives. We succeeded in finding a sixteen-year-old girl whom Geoffrey claimed as his 'cousin' and said he was going to help with her education. She is the daughter of Neville Davy, one of Herbert's Jamaican children. Indeed Geoffrey did make consistent efforts in the years following to pay his cousin's school fees, despite many difficulties in implementing the plan. Was this his attempt at recompense?

PART 6 SUMMARY AND CONCLUSION

Summary

In this book I have told the story of the Davy family of Countess Wear, their Jamaican slave plantations of Topsham, Wear Pen and Heavitree, and the subsequent history of the family. I have made extensive use of the West Indian Slave Registers to extract as much information as I could on the conditions of slavery on the Davy plantations and to learn about individual enslaved people. I have put the story of this family and their enslaved Africans into the context of early nineteenth century slavery in Jamaica under conditions of Amelioration and then Emancipation. I have told how this family divided their time between their plantations in the hills of Jamaica and their home area around the Exe Estuary in Devon, and how some of them eventually took their talents and energy to the new colonies in Australia. I have situated the Davy men within a typology of Devon slave-owners in terms of the size of their compensation, and shown how the proceeds of slavery were used to advance the social status of these men through elite education, and indeed how they were able to make social and scientific contributions because of it. The story reveals the close and enduring friendships between families across the Atlantic which gave them social support in a hazardous world. It also traces present-day descendants through the Windrush era migration to the UK which divided Jamaican families. It ends with the heart-warming story of the meeting of distant 'cousins' from Jamaica and Australia with a promise of much-needed help to a teenage girl.

Conclusion

Not all slave-owners were fabulously rich, living idle lives in splendid country mansions. This story of the Davy family of Countess Wear has shown a middle way, of how an enterprising tenant farming family gradually built up their business capital and know-how and seized the opportunity when it arose to make use of the slave-plantation system to enrich themselves, and in so doing to have a prominent role in founding the newly created society of the Jamaican parish of Manchester, built though it was on racial oppression. Although they made handsome profits, these were not enough to return to England and build themselves extravagant country houses, but it was enough to allow them to live in comfort and to raise their sons to the professional class through their education. It seems that they were talented, hardworking and entrepreneurial so that their next generations made contributions to British society through, for example, leadership in medicine at the RD&E and in the reformed Poor Law, as well as in early Australia through science and medicine.

And not all enslaved people were nameless and faceless. They were individuals with family ties who occupied different roles on the plantations and had different fortunes after they were freed from bondage. With a certain amount of help, as in the free villages for example, some of the formerly enslaved people carved out proud and independent lives for themselves, contributing to their communities in Jamaica or emigrating to build new lives in Britain or North America.

Black and white histories are intertwined – this is surely one message to be taken from the Davy story. We should not be afraid of confronting this past but understand it and grow from it.

APPENDIX

Family trees

Davy family tree 1: The generation who went to Jamaica

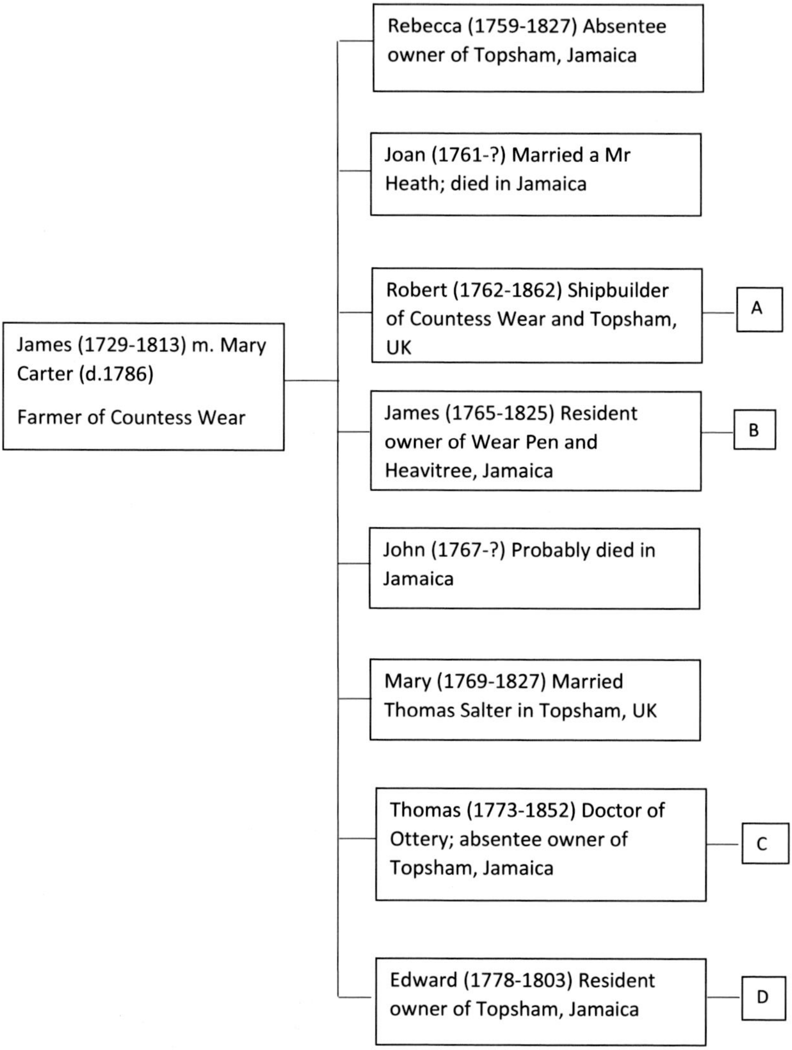

B Davy family tree 2:
Selected descendants of James Davy of Wear Pen

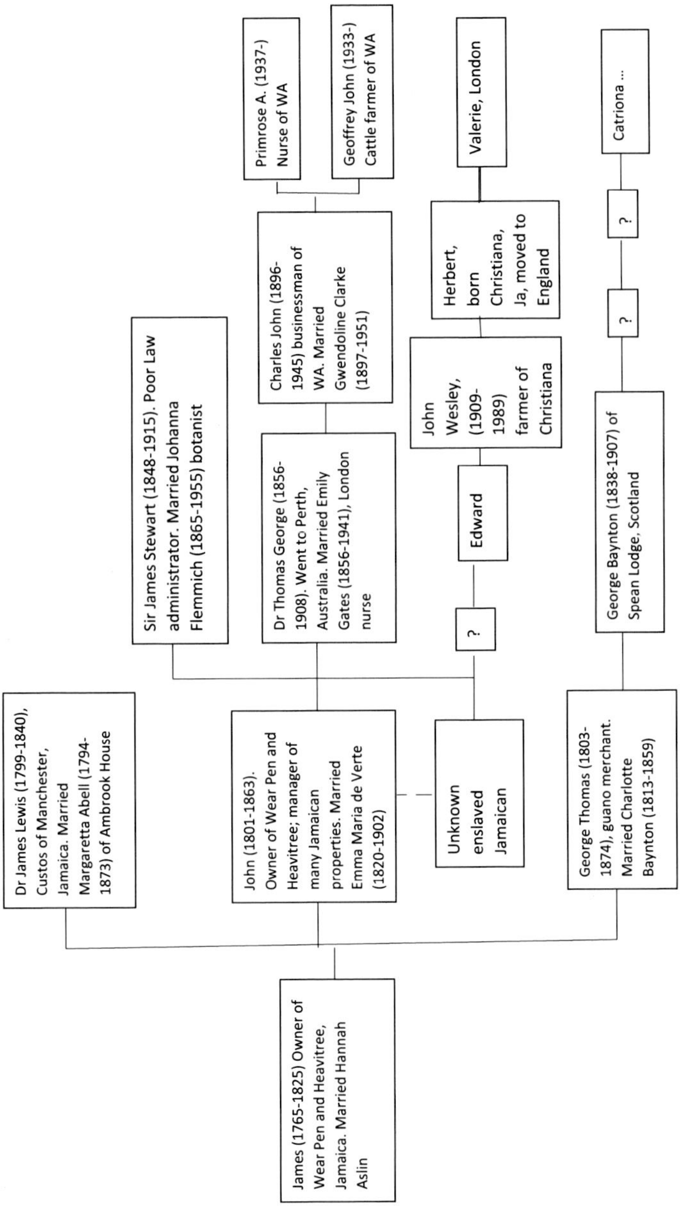

Davy family tree 3: Later generations – selected descendants

A

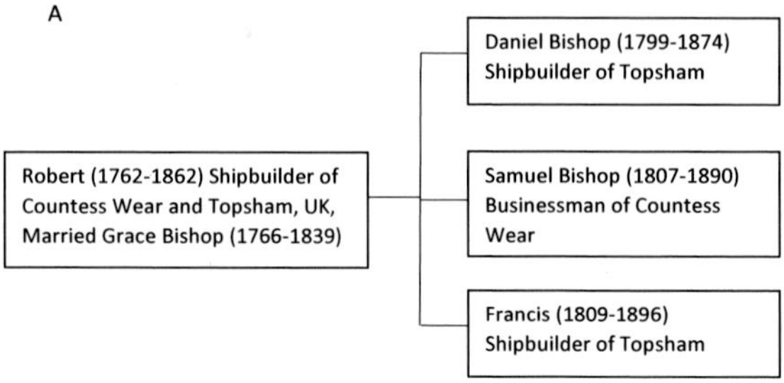

C

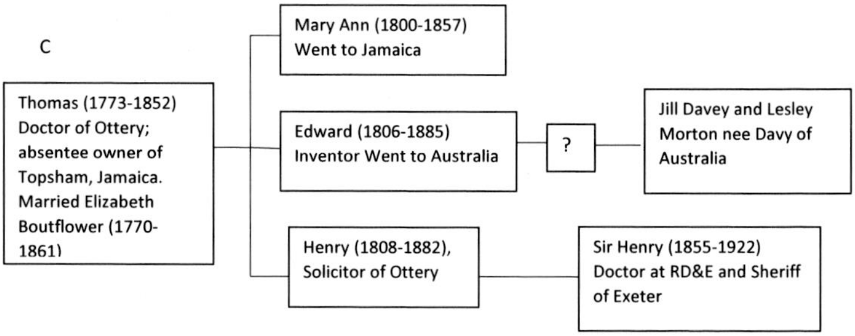

Sale of Prince from William and Isabella Copland to James Davy: transcription of Folio 17

(Partly obscured: Jamaica Feb 1792)

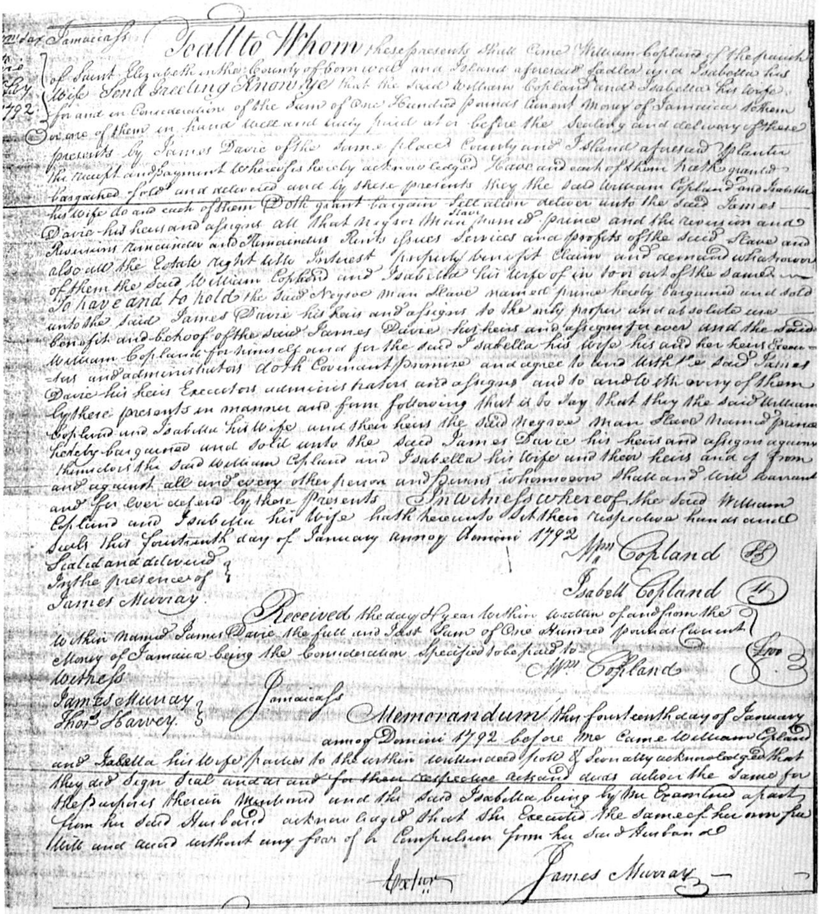

To all to whom these presents shall come William Copland of the parish of Saint Elizabeth in the county of Cornwall and island aforesaid saddler and Isabella his wife Send Greeting Know Ye that the said William Copland and Isabella his wife for and in consideration of the sum of one hundred pound current money of Jamaica to them to one of them in hand well and truly paid at or before the sealing and delivery of these presents by James Davie of the same place County and Island aforesaid planter the receipt and payment whereof is hereby acknowledged Have and each of them hath granted bargained sold and delivered and by these presents they the said William Copland and Isabella his wife do and each of them Doth grant bargain sell alienate and deliver unto the said James Davie his heirs and assigns all that negro man slave named Prince and the reversion and reversions remainder and remainders rents issues services and profits of the said slave and also all the estate Right life interest property benefit claim and demand whatsoever of them the said William Copland and his wife Isabella of in to or out of the same.

To have and to hold the said negro man slave named Prince hereby bargained and sold unto the said James Davie his heirs and assigns to the only proper and absolute use benefit and behoof of the said James Davie his heirs and assigns for ever and the said William Copland for himself and for the said Isabella his wife his and her heirs executors and administrators doth covenant promise and agree to and with the said James Davie his heirs executors administrators and assigns and to and with every of them by these presents in manner and form following that is to say that they the said William Copland and Isabella his wife and their heirs the said negro man slave named Prince hereby bargained and sold unto the said James Davie his heirs and assigns against themselves the said William Copland and Isabella his wife and their heirs and of from and against all and every other person and persons whomsoever shall and will warrant and for ever defend by those presents

In witness whereof the said William Copland and Isabella his wife hath hereunto set their respective hands and seals this fourteenth day of January anno domini 1792

Wm Copland

Isabell Copland

Sealed and delivered in the presence of James Murray

Received the day and year within written of and from the within named James Davie the full and last sum of one hundred pounds current money of Jamaica being the consideration specified to be paid to Wm Copland.

Witness:

James Murray

Thomas Harvey

LOS Deeds Libers 397, folio 17 (source: Island Record Office, Spanish Town, Jamaica)

This document provides firm evidence for James Davy's purchase of an enslaved man, with the date of the transaction and the amount of money paid.

BIBLIOGRAPHY

Main websites for particular facts:

www.ancestry.com

www.familysearch.org

www.jamaicanfamilysearch.com

www.ucl.ac.uk/lbs

Background reading:

Davy, G.J.G. (2013). *The Davy family: Gaius 1633 to Ebony Rae 2012*. Exlibris.

Dunn, R.S. (2014). *A tale of two plantations: Slave life and labor in Jamaica and Virginia.* Cambridge Mass.: Harvard University Press.

Ponsford, C.N. (1988). *Shipbuilding on the Exe.* Exeter: Devon and Cornwall Record Society.

Shepherd, V. and Beckles, H.M. (2000). *Caribbean slavery in the Atlantic world: A student reader.* Kingston, Jamaica: Ian Randle.

Sherlock, P. and Bennett, H. (1998). *The story of the Jamaican people*. Kingston, Jamaica: Ian Randle.

Williams, E. (1944). *Capitalism and slavery.* University of North Carolina Press.